FABULOUS FOOD CONCEPTS

respecting the planet

FABULOUS TO GO

FABULOUS TO BUY

Table of contents 04

Introduction 07

01. Leon 10

02. Burgermeester 18

03. Soepmie 22

04. Kickstand 24

05. Outstanding in the Field 26

06. Marije Vogelzang 36

07. De Kas 42

08. Dogmatic 46

09. Le Pain Quotidien 50

01. Y water 60

02. Bee Raw 68

03. Original Beans 76

04. Dry Soda 78

05. BOS Ice Tea 84

06. Frozen Dutch 88

07. tap water 90

08. LunchSkins 94

09. WB&CO 96

FABULOUS TO SHOP

FABULOUS TO FARM

01. Marqt — 104

02. The People's Supermarket 112

03. Unpackaged — 116

04. Fishes — 120

05. De Vegetarische Slager — 130

06. Mutterland — 132

07. Lindy & Grundy — 136

01. Dakboerin — 142

02. PlantLab — 148

03. Allotinabox — 152

04. Willem & Drees — 160

05. GRO Holland — 156

Credits — 165

Photo credits — 166

Introduction

When people are asked 'what is your idea of a natural food product?', they usually reply that it must be a fresh product, not excessively processed and with as few artificial ingredients as possible. Yet our richly stocked supermarket shelves are more than 90% filled with products that have lost much of their natural character. You can bake biscuits at home from five ingredients, but the packaging on store-bought biscuits lists ten to twenty ingredients that have often been transported from every corner of the globe. Fruit juice is another example: all that is required to make it is pressing, bottling and sterilisation, but many fruit juices are in fact diluted concentrates and a confusing range of juices are available, with added artificial sweeteners and flavourings. For many consumers the food production process has become a black box: often we no longer know to what extent a food product has been processed and transformed. As a result, more and more people are worried about the quality of their food.

Our global food system is also having an impact on our planet. Intensive methods used in agriculture, forestry and fishing are causing irreparable damage to ecosystems. Fertile soil is exhausted and is subsequently washed or blown away, while overfishing threatens important fish species with extinction and distorts the natural equilibrium of our lakes and oceans. Deforestation is on the increase and fertilisers and pesticides are polluting our surface water. In addition to all this, our food production uses a lot of fossil energy. "When we eat, we take in oil and emit greenhouse gases" is food journalist Michael Pollan's stated view on the subject. He has calculated that it currently takes ten calories of fossil fuel to produce one calorie of supermarket food, which is as much as 27 times more than in 1940. Proteins of animal origin (meat, fish and cheese), food transported by air and produce grown in glasshouses heated during the winter are all having a major impact in this area.

Based on the above analysis, concerns are growing over the current food system. People want to make food choices that are more responsible in terms of their own physical health, the sustainability of life on our planet, or both. Locally produced food, seasonal produce, eating less meat, more vegetarian options and growing your own fruit and vegetables are all increasingly commonplace. This kind of sustainable change can only take place if consumers actively seek out food that is environmentally friendly - on a large scale - and producers come up with responses to that demand.

The brands and companies that we have selected for this book are creating those responses. This is not a well-meaning but ultimately pathetic effort by the socks-and-sandals brigade; it is a positive story of modern entrepreneurship.

They hold back from thrusting the negative consequences of the old food system in consumers' faces. Instead, they demonstrate an honest respect for our planet and its inhabitants and inspire enthusiasm among customers by offering products that are tastier, fresher and healthier. They present this reality in beautifully designed stores, inspiring packaging and inventive communication. As a result, they are able to win over less environmentally conscious consumers and create sustainable brands that have the potential to reach the mass market.

Sustainability is being re-cast in a more inspiring mould. You will find this combination in all 30 brands that we have selected for this book. In most cases we have spoken to the founders, seeking to shed as much light on their stories as possible. Naturally, the list of 30 is still a subjective one, and there are many other brands that are not mentioned in the book but perhaps deserve a place in it. What's more, new brands that meet our criteria are emerging almost every day. Who knows, perhaps we will produce a second book one day. Creating this book has been a tremendously inspiring learning experience.

Luster Publishing

FABULOUS TO GO

01. Leon

02. Burgermeester

03. Soepmie

04. Kickstand

05. Outstanding in the Field

06. Marije Vogelzang

07. De Kas

08. Dogmatic

09. Le Pain Quotidien

01
FABULOUS TO GO

Name Leon
URL leonrestaurants.co.uk
Origin United Kingdom

healthy fast food chain sourcing locally

> That is our mission: food should taste good and do you good. And everyone should be able to enjoy it. We call it the good life.

On 26 June 2004 the concept of fast food took on a whole new meaning with the opening of the first Leon restaurant in Carnaby Street, London. Six months later and Leon found itself winner of the "Best New Restaurant in Great Britain Award" from The Observer Food Monthly. Come 2011, there are now some ten Leons dotted around London and one just outside London In Kent. However, the thing that made the people behind Leon really go full ball was the passion and support of their customers who became instant Leon Lovers right from the start. They may not have understood Leon's culinary principles from day one but they kept coming back because Leon's superfood was just yummy.

Years before Leon came to fruition, the three co-founders Allegra McEvedy, Henry Dimbleby and John Vincent – connected through long lasting friendships and family relations – already shared a dream: to bring really good seasonal food to as many people as possible at a fair price.

Allegra had been a chef in a string of famous restaurants such as Robert De Niro's New York restaurant Tribeca Grill. At the time, she was already rebelling against the belief that a chef could only make a difference in high-end restaurants. She wanted to reach more people with good food and began setting up such projects as "The Good Cook" in a community centre in Notting Hill. Henry also used to be a chef before he went into management consultancy, where he met John. Soon after, John and Henry noticed that they had a parallel point of view when it came to the future of food. The trio clicked instantly and began holding regular meetings after their day jobs. After a few years, their abstract ideas took shape and a solid, concrete concept emerged. One by one they left their jobs, committing themselves completely to the Leon ideal.

It is all about starting with the right basic building blocks: our food is as unprocessed and as close to its natural state as possible.

We met Henry at Leon in Carnaby Street and asked him to tell us more about the initial idea behind the concept.

"In our Western world, there is this perception that in order to look after your body, you have to deny yourself. We have been raised with the belief that what is good for you involves some kind of sacrifice and all lovely things - such as brownies - involve some kind of guilt. We passionately hope that Leon food never feels like that. The health thing should seem no more than secondary to our customers who come to enjoy our food. They eat it and feel good about themselves. And that is our mission: food should taste good and do you good. And everyone should be able to enjoy it. We call it the good life."

In what way is Leon food good?

"We read a lot about good food before we began e.g. In Defense of Food: An Eater's Manifesto, by Michael Pollen. There are a number of principles we took into account while developing the Leon menu. It is all about starting with the right basic building blocks: our food is as unprocessed and as close to its natural state as possible. We serve a lot of vegetables and fruits at the peak of their ripeness – because the taste is at its best then - and we favour good carbs such as pulses and whole grains over bad carbs such as white rice. We also use good fats instead of bad fats. When it comes to preparing the food we use olive oil and fresh herbs and spices. And we serve more chicken and fish than red meat.

On our website you can check out a new version of the famous food pyramid that was created by some dissenters at US Harvard. It banishes bad carbs to the smallest part at the top and recommends eating plenty of good carbs and good fats. The food pyramid we grew up with now looks as if it might have been leading us all in the wrong direction: it led to a craze of low-fat diets. Now we know that good fats – found in olive oil, nuts, seeds and oily fish – are essential for your wellbeing and may even play an important role in healthy weight loss."

How do you select your suppliers?

"We only buy ingredients from farms we trust. We select them ourselves and we visit them regularly. This is an enormous amount of work but it is vital to our concept. Our meat for example is Freedom Food endorsed and comes from father and son Basil and Richard at the Gatcombe Farm. They breed animals

> We serve a lot of vegetables and fruits at the peak of their ripeness because the taste is at its best then.

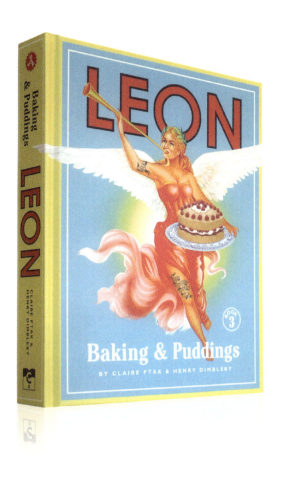

on a unique piece of pasture near the coast. We won the RSPCA Good Business Award in recognition of this. Our fish comes from sustainable shoals, our eggs are free-range. We also buy fair trade and organic products when we believe they are clearly beneficial for health and when we can offer them at a price within reach of everyone, not just the affluent few. Furthermore, we aim to source 70% of our food from the UK and 90% from within the EU. There are areas where we have not reached those targets but we are improving continuously. In January 2010 The Sustainable Restaurant Association awarded us a silver mark. We are very pleased because it recognises the work we have done in the area of sustainability. But we know we are not there yet. In 2011, we are focussing on three things: measuring the water we use and conserving it, increasing our engagement with local communities and increasing the seasonal elements of our menu.

That covers the ingredients and how they are produced. What about the choice of dishes and composing the menu? Who takes care of that?

"Allegra is in charge of developing the seasonal menus but the ideas and recipes are initiated by all of us, the three co-founders and the whole staff. An idea might sit for a while, might even be put to sleep, until Allegra finds the right ingredient or combination to make it work."

Who came up with the name Leon and what does it stand for?

"Well, it is just a beautiful name. When you look at other brand names, certainly in this sector, you always have a kind of description added to it like nutritious, vital, etcetera. We firmly believe this restricts the relationship you can have with something. We just wanted a word that people could

> We only buy ingredients from farms we trust. We select them ourselves and we visit them regularly.

We aim to source 70% of our food from the UK and 90% from within the EU.

relate to and that sounded nice. We wrote lists and lists of names, just names. Leon is the name of John's dad and it is just perfect: it looks beautiful written, it has no place and it could be anything: Spanish, Islamic, Jewish, Christian. Ideal for when we are ready to conquer the world (laughs).

And maybe you have noticed but we do not have a logo: Leon is written in different types and colours. People found this strange at the beginning. But a brand is about a feeling, about an emotion and time has proved us right: when people see one of the hundreds of signatures we have, they know it is Leon, even if we do not mention the name. Moreover, we do not have one baseline. Instead we use these small one liners we put everywhere: just made, packed with love, tastes good, does you good, etc."

The interiors at Leon restaurants are vibrant and full of colour. Are they the work of an architect?

"We created a lot of the interior design ideas ourselves but we had some help from a lovely friend of John's, French designer Bamby Sloan. Every Leon interior is deliberately finished differently. We wanted to create something that could be changed all the time and follow the rhythms of life: a Friday at Leon's can be naughtier than a Monday and summer is different from winter. When you look at other brands, they pride themselves on being the same in summer and in winter, in Tokyo and in London, on Friday and on Monday. We did not want that. As for the practical side of things, the interior is partly based on the fast food 'engine'. Other fast food restaurants have been working on that practicality for decades so why not take the core of that and translate it into our brand. The menu boards and counters are no doubt a familiar reference (laughs)."

Another vital link in the restaurant business is the staff that serves your customers. What are your standards for recruiting?

"At this point in time we have around 200 people working for us. I have hired them all myself and I only have two criteria: when they come to the interview they have to smile and be outgoing. And second: they have to like food. They do not have to be able to cook but they have to like eating. Because you cannot train people how to smile – and customers are entitled to a smile when they walk in – and you cannot train them how to enjoy food. Once those two bases are covered, new recruits undergo training where they learn all about the ingredients and the recipes."

How would you describe Leon's clientele?

Are they healthy food freaks or just your average man (or woman) in the street?

"Over the past few years, Leon has built up a rank and file of very engaged customers: who we believe form the ideal marketing machine. Some of our loyal customers have been eating the Superfood Salad every day since we opened on Carnaby Street. Perhaps these first fans were more health conscious and understood the concept almost straight

We always believed that at some point people would do good food on a worldwide basis and we wanted to be part of that when it happened.

away. To others we had to make the story more accessible than it was in the beginning. For instance, our first menus only listed ingredients in words. When people walked in they would stand in front of the menus with their mouths open. We called it the Carnaby stare (laughs). That prompted us to start working with photos of the dishes. At first we hated the idea of photographing our food; it reminded us of bad pita restaurants. But award-winning food photographer, Jason Lowe, did a great job and made it look delicious."

Besides your loyal customers, how does Leon promote itself? Do you have big advertising budgets?

"We are not big enough – yet – to advertise. It is a pity because I really would like to fight for the mindshare of children and do all the stuff our fast food competitors such as McDonalds do: huge TV-campaigns, bill boarding, etcetera. When it comes to other marketing expressions: we tried working with an ad agency once or twice but it did not suit us. As a founder you want to be in control of what you tell the world. So we prefer working with freelancers, the ones we can sit next to at the computer (laughs)."

What will become of Leon when he grows up? What is he dreaming of?

"We always believed that at some point people would do good food on a worldwide basis and we wanted to be part of that when it happened. We still have a lot of work to do but in a few years we will hopefully be ready to go abroad. Before that we will keep on striving for more food from local suppliers and more sustainability. Recycling has been a tricky one to crack. It is hard to find companies to recycle packaging with food waste on it, and separating different types of waste is another issue. However, we can compost any food wasted in our kitchens, and ran a very successful trial in the summer of 2009 in our Strand restaurant (with the help of juniperfoodwaste.com) where we composted over a quarter of a tonne of waste in the first month. We have now extended this to four more of our restaurants (Carnaby Street, Cannon Street, Ludgate Circus and Regent Street). If the trial continues to be a success we will roll this out to all of our restaurants. We will let you know how it goes.

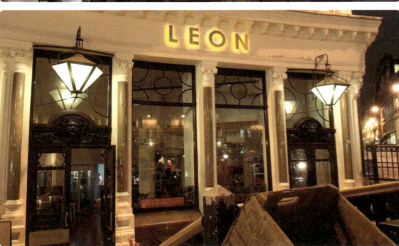

02 FABULOUS TO GO

Name **Burgermeester**
URL **burgermeester.eu**
Origin **The Netherlands**

sustainable hamburger restaurants

The images of healthy grazing cattle adorning the walls of Burgermeester in Amsterdam suggest that they serve more than just a burger. If you come here, you know what you are eating, which fits in perfectly with Burgermeester's philosophy: quality, produced responsibly. It is a new vision of Fast Food created by Dion Eggen, Justus De Nijs and Vincent Van Olphen, three friends who got together in Amsterdam to look for a sustainable combination of both healthy and affordable food.

The Blonde d'Aquitaine cattle are grass-fed and naturally raised. Most of their lives they spend outdoors on a beautiful stretch of protected farmland in the Betuwe region. Everything at Burgermeester is made in-house from scratch, even the ketchup and mayonnaise, using local and seasonal products wherever available. Nice detail: each month creative burger fans are invited to think up a recipe for a new burger of the month. There is a champagne reception for the winner and the burger has a place on the menu.

You can find Burgermeester at three different locations in Amsterdam. The focus is currently on optimising the quality of the existing restaurants, but this formula has a taste for success. We spoke to Justus de Nijs.

How did the idea for Burgermeester come about?

In 2006, I met with two friends from school to brainstorm about what we could do together. All three of us wanted to start a business, and based on our previous work experience the hotel and catering sector seemed a logical choice. Dion had studied hotel management, while Vincent and I had spent one and a half years setting up and running a (small) temporary staff agency for hotel and catering staff. What we wanted more than anything was to do something different.

Vincent told us that he had tasted some incredible burgers in New Zealand during a world tour. So, we were wondering why there were no decent hamburgers to be found in Amsterdam and the surrounding area. That is how the idea came about.

To give us the best chance of achieving our aim – the best, finest burgers, made with sustainable ingredients using traditional methods at an affordable price – we decided to sell burgers and nothing else. Our core business has to be in the foreground. We did not just want to be a glorified snack bar or a cafe where you could also get a burger.

What is the starting point when it comes to selecting ingredients?

Quality comes first. We want to know where every ingredient comes from. We need to have seen it with our own eyes. When we were looking for the best beef we found a farmer in the Betuwe region, and we went to Texel for the lamb. Organic is a quality label and it is a good initiative. Nevertheless, there are many products and ingredients that do not have the label but offer at least the same guarantees of quality and (living)

In fact it is madness that doing business responsibly can still make you stand out from the crowd today.

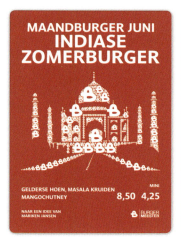

conditions or even better. For products that we cannot (yet) go and see for ourselves, we do have to rely on quality labels. Our fish is MSC approved, our coffee is ecological & fair trade and, as well as many other organic products, we use only organic eggs to make our mayonnaise. We make the ketchup ourselves too. This is not only because we think it tastes better, but also because we know exactly what is in it.

Looking at the meat specifically, how did you find the cows in the Betuwe region?

Through a caterer who is a friend of ours, we found a farmer with a delightful farm in the Betuwe where the animals are treated extremely well. The cattle are scattered widely on this protected farm over about 100 hectares. They live quite freely and eat whatever they wish. This results in excellent meat quality and fits perfectly with our philosophy.

Sustainability is not limited to the food. Can you clarify that?

The great thing about starting your own business is that you are free to do what you think matters. That is true when it comes to offering specific services or designing a menu card. Sustainability and responsible enterprise are personal choices for us, not simply a marketing tool. We do not want to be involved in harmful businesses or do anything that is detrimental to the environment.

That choice goes beyond selecting ingredients. We buy (real) green power, our restaurants are built using materials with a long life, we use as little energy as possible and our staff shirts are made of bamboo and ecological cotton. I think it is a good thing for businesses to make choices in favour of responsible enterprise, not just customers, guest or individuals. In fact, it is madness that doing business responsibly can still make you stand out from the crowd today.

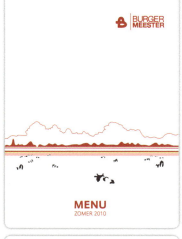

We want to know where every ingredient comes from.
We need to have seen it with our own eyes.

What are your plans for the future? Do you plan to expand the chain?

Everything begins with a dream. Within our first three years we had three restaurants and a production kitchen. After a sprint like that it was time to refine and improve the concept, including the financial aspects.

We like to do as much as we can for ourselves. Of course it would be great if every town and city ended up with a Burgermeester, and we also find the idea of going international very appealing. I think the concept could be successful in other cities within Europe, and perhaps even in New York. These are still dreams; we are not there yet. First we must conquer Amsterdam.

04
FABULOUS TO GO

Name **Soepmie**
URL **soepmie.be**
Origin **Belgium**

organic soup delivered by cargo bike

A sustainable idea does not have to be big to be good. Mieke Dumortier, the founder of Soepmie in Antwerp, has proven that. Soepmie is a contemporary, environmentally friendly version of a lost Flemish profession: the soupman. Every day Mieke rides her bicycle with its cargo box from homes to businesses delivering fresh, homemade organic soups.

Besides soup there is also a savoury salad and a sweet salad every day, and a portion of organic bread if you wish. This is a simple model, but it is particularly efficient from an ecological perspective. There are no CO2 emissions because Soepmie does everything by bicycle, she collects the vegetables from organic farmers in the area and all the soups are vegetarian. Meat and fish both have large impacts on the environment and Mieke never uses them. One particularly positive result of this is that her customers, many of whom are not vegetarians, still choose one meat and fish free meal per day. To limit the amount of waste she encourages her customers to use their own bowls and pots and she serves the soup in those. If they do request a soup bowl, they have to pay extra. Finally, the seasonings and salads are served in pots made from PLA, a biodegradable packaging material based on maize that can be composted.

The concept was created when Mieke took a year off and realised that it was time for a change. She had always wanted to do something active that involved food. Doing it in a sustainable way was a logical consequence. "I am definitely not the one to man the barricades when it comes to sustainability", says Mieke. "I try to be kind to the environment in my own little way and I get very annoyed when I hear that there are so many companies and countries that are still getting it completely wrong. The great thing about my little business is that I can choose to work in the most environmentally friendly way I can, even though it is on a tiny scale, and I feel that my customers value that."

Soup names, such as 'Oh you sweet potato', 'Spring in a bowl' and 'With love from France', are enough to make your mouth water.

05
FABULOUS TO GO

Name **Kickstand**
URL **kickstandbrooklyn.com**
Origin **USA**

barrista's on bicycles serving coffee with the smallest carbon footprint

Aaron Davis, Neal Olsen, Pete Castelein and Ben Schleif, "all midwestern boys who share a lust for the caffeinated life and cycling" are the driving forces behind the mobile pedal-powered coffee concept called Kickstand.

Kickstand's main goal is to make the best possible cup of single-origin coffee with the smallest environmental impact. Two bicycles, a fold-up stand and a manual coffee grinder are about all the Brooklyn-based baristas need to provide New York City coffee fans with sustainable hot and cold coffee.

How did you come up with the idea? What is your philosophy?

We have all been avid cyclists for years and after gaining knowledge as baristas all over NYC and the Midwest, we had an epiphany that the two could be combined: serve the best possible cup of coffee while remaining environmentally sound and spreading bicycle advocacy. We started off in the summer of 2010.

How does it work?

We have two modular, bike-pulled carts that carry everything necessary to grind, brew and serve pour-over coffee as well as cold brewed iced coffee. The carts come together to form a 10 ft wide bar that can be manned by up to three baristas depending on demand. We have cut the top half off a normal hourglass shaped Chemex brewer and that is what we use to make our pour-over hot coffee at the stand. The beans are hand-ground on a cup-by-cup basis. Chemex is a really nice process. It has a much tighter weave of the filter than a lot of normal filters. The flavours and natural oils that get extracted are allowed to come to the surface and really shine.

Who designed your carts?

While the carts were very much a team effort, our own Ben Schleif conceived the design and spearheaded the construction.

You do bicycle deliveries of online orders as well?

This spring we launched our Kickstand Cold Brewed Concentrate. It is distributed at retail stores as well as via our home delivery service, which delivers twice a week by bike messenger. We also pick up empty Kickstand bottles for re-use as part of our bottle exchange programme. Essentially we are what the milkman used to be, but with coffee!

What is this cold brewed coffee concentrate?

Our concentrate is made in a multi-hour cold brew, which allows for a gentle extraction of the coffee and yields a full-bodied, nuanced, coffee concentrate. We use multiple filtration systems to ensure the cleanest, smoothest coffee in your cup. The ingredients are filtered water and specialty coffee roasted within 7 days of the brewing and bottling process. No additives or preservatives are added. It can be used for iced coffee but also for hot coffee, in cocktails and in a plethora of other ways.

How far does Kickstand go in its commitment to sustainability? Is it an all-green concept?

I cannot say it is a purely green concept, given that coffee travels a huge distance before we serve it. However, once the coffee is in our hands, we take great care to make sure our operation is environmentally sound. We do so by transporting all materials by bike and by composting/recycling as much as possible. We use beans from Cafe Grumpy. They source some of the best beans available in New York and have direct relationships with farmers to buy their beans. Fair Trade, Organic, and Rainforest Alliance are some of the certifications their beans get. We put the country, the farm, and the actual roast date on the tag that is attached to our bottle of cold brewed coffee concentrate, so our customers know what they are drinking.

Where does the name kickstand come from?

Literally from "kickstands" on our bicycles and also from the idea that we want to create a place to stand, "kick-it", and have some great coffee.

We had an epiphany that the two could be combined: serve the best possible cup of coffee while remaining environmentally sound and spreading bicycle advocacy.

06 FABULOUS TO GO

Name Outstanding in the Field
URL outstandinginthefield.com
Origin USA

table-to-farm concept: a travelling outdoor restaurant

Imagine a table, several metres long, either straight or curved but always perfectly situated in a field, in the woods or on the beach, with folded wooden chairs and white tablecloths, completely in harmony with the environment. That is the trademark of Outstanding in the Field, a restaurant without walls founded in 1999 by cook/artist Jim Denevan. He is now one of the pioneers of the farm-to-table movement. Or should we say table-to-farm, because he brings the table and his guests back to the source, to the place where the ingredients come from. He does this because of his deep respect for small farmers and all the other people who work hard to bring genuine products to the market. The ingredients are worked into complete dishes by well-known chefs from the region and everyone eats together at this shared table: guest, farmer, winemaker, baker,... Each year Jim and his team criss-cross North America in an old red and white Flxible bus, looking for the stories behind the ingredients. We spoke to Jim during his first journey through Europe, at the Vollenhoven estate in the Netherlands, where we took our places for a culinary adventure.

What is the story behind the concept?
The idea goes back to my brother's farm, something I was very familiar with from my childhood. My brother, Bill Denevan, is an organic farmer. He is 14 years older than me. I got to know his farm when I was a teenager. What he does is very direct and meaningful. Farmers are important people who deserve to be recognised and appreciated.

When I became a chef, there was a growing interest in knowing where the food was coming from. Restaurants started mentioning the name of the farms on their menu. Customers liked it when a menu described who made the cheese, where the fish came from, where the animals were raised... Maybe it is because people in cities do not have their own garden or are separated from agriculture, from nature. And of course, my brother's farm was one of those farms. In 1998 we started organising farm-to-table dinners: we brought the farmers into the restaurant where they would talk about their products and guests could ask questions. Chefs get a lot of attention, so why not spend a little time with the farmers. Maybe it will even make you understand more of what a chef does. One year later in 1999, I thought if we could place the table on the farm, put it where the food comes from and be surrounded by the ingredients, that would take it a step further than farm-to-table. That was the beginning of table-to-farm dining and Outstanding in the Field.

What is your mission?
Culturally, food is so powerful and meaningful. It is associated with so many metaphors: the concept of the harvest, the seasons. When people come to a good restaurant, they want to enjoy well-prepared food and good wine, but they also want to have recognition of where they are in time and place. The part about time is that certain vegetables, fish and meat are available at a certain time of year; it is a way for people to acknowledge the seasons. When we started, I definitely believed that it would catch

I always want it to be one table. It can curve or it can be straight, but it needs to fit in with the environment.

on culturally and that people would copy what we do. And that was the idea from the beginning, because I felt that if you put a table out in the field, in that place where the food comes from, that visually, the connection between the harvest and enjoying a meal would be so powerful that people would want to do it all over the world.

Globally there clearly is a growing awareness about local sourcing and sustainable food production. Agriculture is moving into the cities. What is you view on that?

I was invited to speak at a Conference (Pink) in the Netherlands. One of the themes, and something I have been thinking about, was that in a technological society people want to pay more attention to what is directly in front of them. Through technology they have the ability to live in a global society, which is fulfilling in many ways and interesting and fascinating. However, because of that powerful attention that is taken to places that are very far away, the things that are in front of us become more desirable than they would have been 15 or 20 years ago when life was more immediate. Nostalgia for a past when people lived in agrarian societies, when they lived on the farm and celebrated the harvest together, that is definitely one aspect of this interest. As I mentioned before, people want to be set in time and place. Place meaning the physical world they inhabit, things they see from day to day. And time, meaning seasons and the recognition of the passage through life from being younger to getting older. People need a connection. They do not want to be alienated from their surroundings.

Did it increase the success of Outstanding in the Field?

Over the past 3 or 4 years it has really taken off. But you know, to some extent I was attempting to change culture. I saw that things were changing and that at some point an audience would be very pleased to hear these ideas and to be able to sit down at this table and share communally what comes from the ground and what comes from people who work to produce food. And now in North America, we have been to 41 states, we serve almost 12,000 people every year, and they come back year after year. We have crossed North America seven times. Many, many events. So it has become more popular, yes. All over the world those things are becoming more important to people.

What is the story of the table?

I always want it to be one table. It can be curved or it can be straight, but it has to fit in with the environment. Which is somewhat like the artwork that I do: the placement of the table needs to respond to the conditions of the day. There is the composition of the table and the way it looks, and there are the weather conditions that force choices. And of course, it is the communal table of everyone dining together. People can meet people they do not know. There is no assigned seating, so they do not know who they are going to be sitting with that day. People have become separated and because of that they start to fear people they do not know. They only want to talk to people they are familiar with, who have the same attitudes, the same beliefs. I think it reassures people, that you do not have to be afraid of people you do not know. At our table on the farm everyone is invited; guests, farmers, fishermen, cheese makers… they all dine together.

> When we started, I definitely believed that it would catch on culturally and that people would copy what we do.

As an artist you draw huge sand sculptures on beaches or in deserts. Is there a connection with Outstanding in the Field?

In the sense that it exists for the same amount of time, yes. Where we put the table, that morning there was nothing there. It is a bit like the tide. The table is placed in the environment to be there for 4 or 5 hours. We always clean up the same night and then everything is gone, from the beginning to the end. That aspect of it is similar to the artwork. It disappears when the tide turns. But also in the composition, why there is a curved or a straight line, however it fits. I get pretty excited about getting that just right. And there is a bit of theatre to it. The guests do not see the table when they arrive. They get a tour, see the farm, hear the farmers' stories, get a feel for the land where the food is coming from, and then they come upon it.

Guests are asked to bring their own plates. Why is that?

A lot of 'Events', and catering in general, have been very codified: the same white plates, the same tent, the same food, who knows where it came from. It has become stale, bland, boring. We want to emphasise all along the way that everything has a story to it. If it were just from the rental company, it would be about the rental company. But since people bring their own plate, and of course since the group of people is diverse, the plates are going to be diverse. Some of them will be expensive and maybe others will be made by someone's children. We have seen every kind of plate. We did it at the very first events because we wanted to emphasise that this was not going to be like any other event.

Ingredients are sourced locally, but are they organic as well?

Generally, that is the theme of what we do. Probably in Europe biodynamic agriculture is pretty strong. But in the US it has been hard for small farmers to get organically certified because of all the paperwork. A number of farmers who use organic methods cannot call their food organic because they do not have the papers.

Have you been working with the same farmers over the years?

There are quite a few that we have returned to year after year. Some of them we visited maybe 7 times, some chefs came back six or seven times. We actually try to change, but it is hard to do so because we start to like them.

We like to have 50 per cent new and 50 per cent places we have been. So it is kind of a mix. Some are CSA's (Community-supported agriculture), sometimes they grow for the farmer's markets, sometimes they grow for restaurants. Generally, we prefer diverse farms because they are more interesting than a farm that grows one thing. It is so much of what the events are about, that people, during the tour, can see many things growing. Big farms are not so interesting to visit.

Travelling from May through October? How do you prepare for the tour?

We figure out whom the staff are going to be in December-January and then they all come into California and work for a few weeks as we prepare to cross the country. Generally, there are eight people on the team. They are from all over: Chicago, Portland, Canada, the Netherlands, Germany, Switzerland,... Two or three of us are from California, but it is nicer to have a mix of people. We have about 25 events in California in May and June. They are closer to where I and some of the staff live. May and June does not involve so much travelling, we just drive. We do not live out of the bus because it is close enough. On the 1st of July, we get on the bus and start travelling all over North America. So normally, it is July, August, September, October and a little bit of November. This is our first time in Europe.

Do you still work as a chef at the events?

In the early years, I was the chef. Now I only do the first event every year. When we are travelling we pick a guest chef that is notable in the region, someone who knows the farmers and knows the sources and ingredients. They act as ambassador of the event. They are the one to showcase whatever is available.

How do you promote the event? How do you reach the guests?

The guests can always look forward to the tickets being sold on the first day of spring. That is what we do consistently every year. We have a mailing list of more than 50,000 people. We send them notice of events that are coming up. We are just about to send a notice of all our events happening in the wintertime. And we have had a lot of press attention.

Europe now? What is next?

First we go back to America. We are in Hawaii and Florida in the winter. We will make a special trip to go to these places when the weather is best. It is too warm now. We do the Southern hemisphere in January, February and part of March, when it is their harvest season. We have 16 events from Africa to Australia and Asia. And then we start again in May. So it is going to be more full year round. I probably will not be able to go to all these event, that is too much. We will see.

What is the most rewarding part for you?

When farmers, fishermen, cheese makers are elevated and more highly regarded, when there is more respect for everyone associated with food, it elevates culture and makes it more powerful for people when they do enjoy a meal. It is good for guests, farmers and chefs to become closer. But also the fact that everyone is sitting together and celebrating a meal together. That it is a place to talk about ideas and the world with people you never knew you were going to meet that day. In Europe, people really respond to the emphasis we place on the different aspects of a meal. I think the mix of the things that take place creates a feeling of satisfaction at the end.

> I thought if we could place the table on the farm, put it where the food comes from and be surrounded by the ingredients, that would take it a step further than farm-to-table.

> We just really want to bring the table to other places and inspire people to do their own version and copy what aspects of it they think are sensible for their culture.

In Europe you have to build it from scratch?

It is hard in a way, kind of like the early days. In North America, we have been on TV. Millions of people have seen it. But it is interesting to see that the people and the press in Europe are following. Some dinners are full, others are half full. But I think it is better that way. We would rather have it somewhat low-key and not have huge expectations in the beginning. It is more of a challenge, of course, but that is part of what we do. North America is so stable. We sell more than 90 per cent of the tickets all on one day, for the whole season. In the last 3 or 4 years it has been amazing, the demand is so great.

We just really want to bring the table to other places and inspire people to do their own version and copy what aspects of it they think are sensible for their culture.

07 FABULOUS TO GO

Name Marije Vogelzang
URL marijevogelzang.nl
Origin The Netherlands

> Eating design is to design from the verb 'to eat'

'eating' designer

Marije Vogelzang is a product designer who has chosen an unusual product as her material: eating. She calls herself an eating designer, not a food designer, because she starts from the verb 'to eat': "Eating design is to design from the verb 'to eat'."

She does not limit herself to the form in which the food is served, but looks beyond it to its origin, preparation, history and the associated culture. For her, the form is just one way of telling a story.

Marije never sits still. Working from her mobile design studio, Marije Vogelzang comes up with remarkably original eating concepts. Meanwhile she travels all over the world to give inspiring lectures on her philosophy of eating. And she writes books. For Marije, sustainability is not the starting-point, it is something quite self-evident. "How can you create a beautiful design if you cannot execute it sustainably?"

You are an eating designer. What exactly does that mean?

I was trained as a product designer at the Design Academy in Eindhoven. During my studies I discovered that you can use food as a material for design. Once you start doing this you discover that food is much more than a material. Food is rooted in all human cultures, and there is a very rich 'eating' history. Above all, eating is psychology. It is a very interesting subject when you talk about sustainability. And there is no other material that comes as close to human beings as food. You put my designs inside your body.

For me, it is really about the verb, about 'eating' rather than just the 'food' itself. That is why I talk about eating design rather than food design, because that term would imply that I design the food itself, but I think that food has already been perfectly designed by nature.

As an eating designer I create concepts for hotels, restaurants and other businesses that involve eating, I work for hospitals and the food industry and I write books. The Broodtrommelboek or Lunchbox Book (ideas for a surprising lunchbox) and EAT LOVE (an overview of 10 years of eating design) that is now in its third revised edition, and there are two more books on their way.

What is your perspective on food and sustainability?

Food is the basis for our existence. At the survival level and at every other level above that, eating gives colour and meaning to our lives. Everyone needs food, and it is the biggest industry on earth. For me, it is interesting to look at all the problems in the world today that relate to food. The sea is being emptied of fish and we eat things without having any idea who made them, what is in them or how you should really prepare them. We pay far too little for our food and we no longer take time to eat it or else we eat in solitude. All these things are alarming, but they also offer an inspiration for people to think creatively and do something about it. As a creative person that is exactly the kind of thing you should be working on. Sometimes solutions can be found simply through a different way of thinking. And food is a very rich subject.

You cannot create a beautiful design and then not execute it sustainably.

Sustainability is no longer the key issue for me, it is the self-evident result of thinking positively. You cannot create a beautiful design and then not execute it sustainably. For example, I think it is great that we have a worm box at Proef (a box containing composting worms that make compost from the garden and kitchen waste).

You have a restaurant called Proef in the Westerpark in Amsterdam. When and how did Proef come into being?

In 2004 we started up Proef in Rotterdam as an eating design studio and a place to eat. In 2006 we expanded into Amsterdam, but Proef Rotterdam no longer exists.

The idea of combining an eating design studio with a restaurant is interesting, but it never really worked. These are actually two completely different business processes. It is better to make it accessible to the public. Now I do my design work without a fixed location. On the road, at home, in the shower...

What is the Proef concept?

Proef is an excellent restaurant where we work with organic seasonal products and traditional suppliers. It is a place where you share your food with the other people at your table, because sharing is an essential part of the eating process. I think it is a shame that most restaurants give you just one plate per person and you have to eat it all yourself. I prefer the Asian way of eating, where the food all arrives on a large tray in the middle of the table. With just a few small changes you can create a remarkable effect. I design the menu together with the chef. We also have delicious organic cocktails with edible flowers from our herb garden and we have a superb brood of chickens scratching around. I wanted a place where I would enjoy going out to eat myself. The food at Proef is simple, pure and tasty, served in a relaxed picnic environment. We serve coffee in empty jam pots and our emphasis is on (forgotten) vegetables. These are served on the cutting boar. Our table settings are a mixture of second hand items. It is quite simply a lovely, unconventional place.

What is your starting-point when it comes to selecting suppliers and products?

The supplier must have tasty products, they must be special and sustainability is also a factor. Diny Schouten, for example, is a former journalist who used to write about food and forgotten foods. Some time ago she started a business making pâté from home. Now she has rented a butcher's shop and has magically transformed herself into a pie maker. She selects her pigs herself and

processes them from head to tail. These are the initiatives and stories that I like, and the pâté is truly wonderful.

Have you also used sustainable materials in your interior design?
We did not have a very large budget when we opened Proef in Amsterdam, so a lot of things are recycled anyway. The new kitchen, however, is mostly made from FSC certified wood.

Proef has its own vegetable garden. What have you got in the garden?
To be honest I have to tell you that it has become more of an herb garden. It is quite labour-intensive and you need to plant a lot of carrots if you want to serve carrots from your own garden to your guests for a whole week.

Can you tell us more about the famous Proef cocktails?
We have some remarkable cocktails with fine-sounding names like Rabarbarella and Full Frontal Flower Shower. I thought it would be fun to come up with some cocktails that are completely different from what you normally see in bars and restaurants. These often contain edible flowers, but for example you may find some frozen peas too.

Sustainability is everywhere in your work. Can you give a few examples of projects.
Oh dear, I have done so many. The Urban Eco Dinner, for example, where we draw attention to all the 'free' food that is available to pick and find in the city, such as weeds, mushrooms, nuts and pigeons. I did a dinner where the food was cooked under your table in a 'hay box'. That is one way of saving energy. I have served ham and melon from different countries on a painter's palette, with 5 varieties of ham and 5 varieties of melon, with a slip of paper underneath the ham showing the distance the ham and melon had travelled. That allows the guests

I make designs that end up in the toilet

to taste for themselves whether they prefer ham and melon from far away or from nearby. Then we had the tap water tasting event, with tap water from the 12 provincial capitals of the Netherlands. The aim of this was to make people aware of the specific character of tap water by treating it like wine. It really does taste quite different in every city! At Proef we do not have any bottled water; we only serve (free) delicious Amsterdam tap water. Another project is the Roots dinner: root vegetables are harvested and then baked in clay (earth) so that they become sculptures. The guests have to break the clay with a hammer so that they can eat the root vegetables. We then give them the clay to compost their gardens so that they can grow new root vegetables.

I like to see nothing left over after a dinner. That is why I like working with food as a designer. There is never anything left over.

You were involved in the pop-up restaurant Go Slow Cafe, an initiative by Droog Design. What is the idea behind this concept?

I must have been working with Droog since 2004. We have done a number of different projects. They had the basic idea for the Go Slow Cafe and I took it further. We have been in Milan, Tokyo, Rotterdam, London and New York.

The idea is that in this hectic time, the meaning of luxury has shifted. In the past, luxury meant expensive things that you could only buy if you had a lot of money. Nowadays more and more people can afford those things and there are a lot of fakes on the market. Today the real luxuries are time, attention, love, etc. Those are things you cannot buy. The Go Slow Cafe is a place where older people serve you. When you arrive you take off your shoes and they give you a huge pair of slippers. You have to shuffle along carefully in those slippers, and you clean the floor as you go. You receive a personal welcome from an elderly lady or gentleman who shows you to your place. There is a simple menu, made using good quality products. The elderly people place the food in front of you with their own hands. The cream is beaten by hand, the nuts are cracked by hand, the orange juice is squeezed by hand, etc. The idea is that all the care lavished on those things is in the food and it is as if you absorb all this when you eat it. Those elderly people serve you very slowly and with tremendous love. It is like being at home with your own grandpa or grandma. It is a performance. In New York we presented a Distance Menu. This was a cutting board with a series of circles ranging in size from large to small. The largest circle contained food produced within a radius of five miles from the location in question. The second, smaller circle contained food produced within a radius of 20 miles and so on. Finally, at the end, there are very small specks of food from the other side of the world.

Do you only cook with products that are produced/sourced sustainably?

Not necessarily. It is mainly about creating the experience for our guests and the kilometre eater (the cutting board) gives them an insight into where the food comes from. It does make sense that the food should be sustainable, but that is not the top priority. In addition it is sometimes difficult to find the right products from the right area.

What is your ambition for the future? Where do you want to go with the studio Marije Vogelzang?

I want to put Eating Design on the menu. That does not mean that I am going to do many more projects, but rather that I want to look more closely at what is going on in the world in terms of eating and creative thinking. That does not necessarily have to be aimed at designers or artists. For example there are some old people's homes where they are doing some great things such as combining food from the past with music from the past. This seems to make a huge improvement in quality of life for older people. I would like to research and bring together initiatives like that. I travel a lot and see many things, and I would find it interesting to shed more light on other people's work. I am also working on my next book and of course I am continuing to do projects. I am currently working as an SWS (Self-employed Without Staff). I want to be a free person again.

No other material comes as close to human beings as food. You put my designs inside your body.

08
FABULOUS TO GO

Name: De Kas
URL: restaurantdekas.nl
Origin: The Netherlands

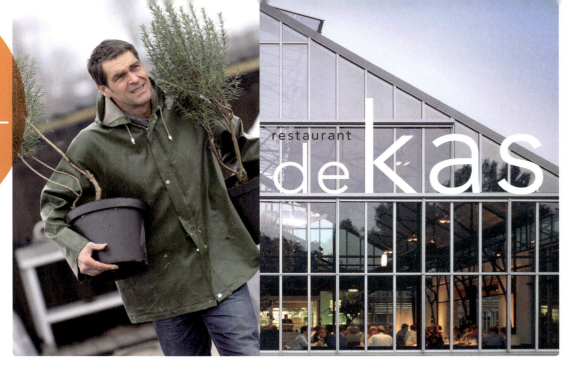

greenhouse restaurant serving vegetables, herbs and edible flowers from its private nursery

Since 2001 De Kas (The Greenhouse) has been occupying a delightful location in Amsterdam: a restored greenhouse almost 100 years old in the middle of Frankendael Park. Owner Gert Jan Hageman, who earned a Michelin star as a top chef in a previous life, saved this dilapidated treasure from demolition and gave it a new lease of life: a restaurant with its own nursery where the dining guests enjoy views of the surrounding greenhouses and garden. You can literally see where your food comes from and the produce harvested every day goes directly onto your plate. And yet, Gert Jan Hageman did not really find his place until he left the kitchen and took over the running of the nursery in 2008. Since then, he has been going out every morning to sow, plant, tend and harvest. In his blog 'News from the Country' he regularly reports with childlike enthusiasm on his experiences as a farmer.

2 June 2011: "...We are harvesting an abundance of flowers: pod flowers, nasturtiums, marigolds, violets, borage, germander, onion flowers, flowering cabbage and mustard, rocket, too numerous to mention. The drought has given us a few headaches, and so has the heat. The lettuces are not coming up as tasty and juicy as I had hoped, some of the plants are in trouble and others are shooting up too fast. That is where the professional stands out from the amateur gardener, and I can see that I do lack a lot of experience. On the other hand we are very enthusiastic, which compensates for that. The team, in the Beemster and Amsterdam, works hard to produce lots of beautiful things and deliver them to the kitchen; I often think to myself: what could be better than this?"

What motivated you to start a concept like De Kas after working as a top chef for so many years?

It was my wife. She saw that I was beginning to show some wear and tear - to put it delicately - and offered me a sabbatical. That period of rest was like a revelation: I suddenly had the dream of opening a restaurant in a greenhouse and growing my own vegetables. Very simple, no more complicated messing about, fabulously fresh and easily recognisable food from the immediate environment. A kitchen where daylight pours in from all sides and chefs enjoy themselves every day working with whatever the season has brought in. The idea seems obvious, but I spent twenty years surrounded by white tiled walls and under the strip lights before it came to me.

It is a splendid location. How did you find it?

Another miracle. The location found me. This former nursery greenhouse dating from 1926 which belonged to the Amsterdamse Handelskwekerij (Amsterdam Commercial Nursery) had been crumbling there for years. Thanks to a tip from the Amsterdams Grondbedrijf (Amsterdam Land Company)

I was able to save it from demolition. With a great deal of luck and help from the local council, friends and family we have succeeded in rebuilding this eight metre high glass structure.

Can you explain the concept? How does De Kas work?

The concept is simple: fresh, local and friendly. Every day we serve one menu with the very best seasonal ingredients you can think of. We harvest every morning and the produce is worked into our dishes the same day. The next day we start again from scratch. Vegetables and herbs from our own nursery, where I rule the roost, form the backbone of our Mediterranean country cuisine, along with the best organic meats, the best MSC fish (MSC is a label for sustainably caught fish) and superbly fresh ingredients from local farmers. That is because we cannot grow everything ourselves.

What is the philosophy of De Kas?

We grow organically and only use responsibly caught fish with the MSC label and animal-friendly meat. Everything comes from the immediate area and we follow the seasons from day one. We try to take our responsibilities on board, not only for our employees but also beyond that wherever we can.

What is your working day like? Do you still spend time in the kitchen?

I get up at six. Harvesting begins at seven o'clock. Then we work in the garden in the Beemster. We have a large arable field about 10 km outside Amsterdam where we grow seasonal vegetables outdoors. I take time out from this to visit De Kas. In the evenings I cook for the family at home, then reply to my emails and go to bed at 23.00. I am afraid it does not sound very exciting.

I have completely stopped working as a chef. Despite my Michelin star I have had enough now and there are other people who can do it better than me - at least they think they can.

How is the menu designed?

Every week I make a list of what is available in the nursery. After discussing this with Ronald Kunis and Meindert Heijer, the executive chef and head cook, we then buy in meat, fish, etc. All that remains is to taste a few wines to go with it. Simplicity and recognisability, that is what De Kas is all about. Vegetables, herbs, vegetables, herbs, vegetables, herbs...

What vegetables and herbs do you grow yourselves?

It is a very long list. Just about anything you can think of. If there is something we do not have, we buy it from our environmentally friendly farmers, and we have now developed a long-term relationship with them. Our highlights are tomatoes, an extensive range

> We try to take our responsibilities on board, not only for our employees but we go beyond that wherever we can.

of herbs and spices, different varieties of basil, edible flowers and particularly delicious strawberries. For all other products we seek out the best suppliers. Our sourdough bread comes from an organic baker, our pasta arrives fresh from an Italian in Amsterdam and we discovered our rice on a culinary trip in Spain.

After running De Kas for 10 years, what stands out for you?
Up to now it has been great fun, with just a few moments of stress.
The future still looks very bright to me. I am not finished with this by a long way.

Simplicity and recognisability, that is what De Kas is all about.

09
FABULOUS TO GO

Name **Dogmatic**
URL **dogmatic.com**
Origin **USA**

Dogmatic is a healthy, sustainable and creative approach to the age-old hot dog.

healthy and sustainable sausage dogs

DOGMATIC ♥ YOU.
AND EVERY DAY WE LOVE CERTAIN PEOPLE EVEN MORE.

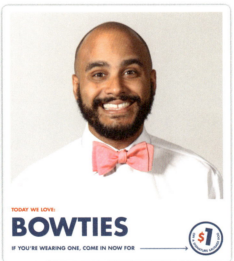

Dogmatic began in 2006 as a food stall in a park in New York's West Village. Thanks to an enthusiastic investor it was upgraded in 2008, relocating to permanent premises opposite the farmer's market on Union Square.

The original concept came from Andrew Deitchmann, entrepreneur and co-founder of creative agency Mother New York.

Dogmatic is a healthy, sustainable and creative approach to the age-old hot dog. This might sound contradictory but the commitment is sincere: "they are Dogmatic about good food". Only natural, perfectly fresh ingredients are used, and animal welfare is taken into account when selecting individual farms. Nutritional value is also carefully monitored, which is quite an achievement in itself, in the fast food sector. At Dogmatic they want you to eat something 'good' and walk out feeling 'good' too.

A large mural depicts the whole story from organic farmer to Dogmatic Sausage Dog. This is a hot dog with a message.

The sausage dogs are prepared using the sophisticated Dogmatic Gourmet Sausage System. Traditionally made baguettes are sliced half-open and impaled on iron spikes so that they are toasted from the inside out. The roll is then filled with a hot sauce that is made in-house, followed by a choice of sausage. No concessions are made when it comes to the quality and origin of the meat. They only work with small farmers from the local area who raise their animals naturally and responsibly; cows that only eat grass, free-range chickens, free-grazing sheep, happy pigs and organic turkeys. The meat that is made into Dogmatic sausages is pure and contains no hormones, antibiotics, nitrates

or preservatives. Dogmatic is primarily about what is good: both for the environment and for you.

Dogmatic aims to convince as many people as possible of their Good Food philosophy, and it does this in its own original way, 'with love'. In June 2011 they organised a promotional campaign on the theme of "Dogmatic Loves You". Over a period of one month there was a focus on a different specific group of customers every day, appreciating them just for who they are. These included men with pigtails, bow ties or curled moustaches, nannies, people with red hair and people wearing pink socks. Anyone who met the description was offered a discount or a free sausage dog. The campaign could be followed online at dogmaticlovesyou.com and was conceived by Mother New York.

Dogmatic is a small, stylish restaurant. The entire front wall is made of glass, which creates a light, open feeling inside. The interior has intentionally been kept simple to avoid distracting attention from the food. If you eat in the restaurant, you share a table in the form of a butcher's block with other hot dog lovers. A large mural depicts the whole story from organic farmer to Dogmatic Sausage Dog. This is a hot dog with a message.

> No concessions are made when it comes to the quality and origin of the meat.

10 FABULOUS TO GO

Name Le Pain Quotidien
URL lepainquotidien.com
Origin Belgium

'Daily Bread' served at a communal table

Less is more – that is one of Alain's slogans. Less choice but more quality. Less ingredients in the sandwich, so you can really taste the full intensity of whatever is on top.

In 1990 the first branch of bakery/café Le Pain Quotidien opened in the centre of the flourishing fashion district of Brussels. Founder Alain Coumont was running a restaurant at the time but could not find the right bread to serve with his meals. He wanted traditional artisanal bread, like the bread his grandmother used to knead by hand when he was a child. He wanted a firm crumb and a hard crust. So he set to work himself, using the ingredients that still form the essence of Le Pain Quotidien: stoneground organic flour, salt and water.

20 years later there are more than 150 branches throughout the world, both fully owned and franchised, but Coumont is still following his gut feeling. He remains the creative, visionary force behind Le Pain Quotidien. Vincent Herbert, who has been CEO of the slow fast food chain since 2003, is his pragmatic opposite number. He keeps an eye on the figures. They understand and complement each other perfectly. Where Coumont stops, Herbert takes over.

The concept has not changed. It has always been about friends and strangers enjoying honest, healthy 'Tartines'* together at a communal table. Sharing your Daily Bread is still the starting-point for Le Pain Quotidien, all over the world.

*A tartine is an open sandwich. The name comes from the French tartiner, which means "to spread".

What is the concept of Le Pain Quotidien?

Le pain Quotidien - French for 'The Daily bread' - is a bakery/café where people gather at a communal table for breakfast, brunch or lunch. Le Pain Quotidien serves simple, organic and elegant 'slow fast food' like soup, salads, tartines, homemade pastries and handmade organic bread. The menu includes many vegan and vegetarian options.

LPQ is a Belgian brand, but the head office has been registered in the US since 2004. Why is this?

We had some good owned branches in the US – in Belgium we were already franchise-only by then – and everything was right there: the brand, our own people. So the US seemed to be a better base from which to develop

franchising further. When we opened a new branch we were able to send good people from our own team in the US to the various countries, so we could guarantee a better level of support. Now we have more owned branches in Europe again. We bought back France, for example, so now we can support new start-ups from Europe too.

Who is the LPQ customer?

65% are women between 28 and 45. We sometimes call them bobos: "bourgeois bohemiens". Originally we were only looking for residential locations, but now we also open branches in business districts and suburbs. That is what allowed men to find their way to LPQ too. A business lunch at LPQ gives you energy. Our menu is quite limited. We keep it simple and that makes it easy for people. People like this, even though they may not realise it. They feel relaxed while they are here and they are full of energy when they leave. Less is more – that is one of Alain's slogans. Less choice but more quality. Less ingredients in the sandwich, so you can really taste the full intensity of whatever is on top.

Who are the driving forces behind LPQ today?

Alain Coumont (Founder) and I (Vincent Herbert, CEO) are. While Alain focuses on the creative part of the concept, I define its growth strategy and look after its business execution. In addition, Alain ensures that the concept stays close to its roots whereas I project the growth of the company. This dichotomy is essential to stable growth.

Is Le Pain Quotidien still evolving?

Everything happens very gradually in this enterprise. For example, Alain is experimenting with veganism, but we do not want to 'impose' this. It must not become a dogma. The art is to make sure that consumers do not immediately notice it. Our authenticity is too important to allow that. On the other hand, we must not pay too much attention to that authenticity or spend our time worrying about it. It is more of a gut feeling about the way we should be: Alain's gut feeling.

Alain is superb at finding 'prophets', people who can continue to pass on his message. That gives him space to evolve and be creative. My job is to put all his crazy ideas on a timeline and look at what we can do now and what we should leave in the drawer. We work on the basis of five-year business plans.

Can you say a little more about the growth strategy?

We do not want to grow too fast. The biggest question I ask myself every day is: what is optimal growth? If we grow too fast, we risk losing sight of our brand. We do not want to grow too large, we want to remain strong. Growth must take place organically. It is a conscious choice between being 'big' or 'great'. We do not want to lose our honesty. It is our ambition to truly enjoy every opening and every day at work. If we had to open 100 branches a year, we would not enjoy it any more. This is an adventure and it should stay that way. Everything is in balance and we still have time for our family and friends.

> The secret of its success resides in the continuous effort of the management to stay true to the roots of the concept and its values: conviviality, authenticity, quality, and simplicity.

Our philosophy influences every part of the way we do business, from the food we serve to the design of our stores to the materials we use. It is good for our bodies, our communities, and our earth.

To what extent is the 'Belgian' character put across in other countries?

We do not emphasise that at all. All our values are Belgian, but they also belong to the whole world: take time, find a balance in your life, show respect, stay in touch with yourself and with other people, eat sensibly, take time to eat. If people do find out that we are Belgian, that probably makes the brand even stronger.

Who works at LPQ and how are these people trained?

'Authenticity through our people' is an important project. We do focus on that a lot. The profile for our staff is Alain's profile: a simple, civilised person, simply dressed and not very conspicuous. Someone who is genuinely friendly and talks to people. Not a fake, but someone authentic and real. It is very difficult to find people like that, and that is another reason why our growth is quite slow. This is a vision that has to come from above; that is the way every person at every level has to 'be'. Our employees should feel that working here helps them to become a better person. If we can achieve that, we can develop people who feel good here, work hard and stay with us.

Recruitment cannot be delegated; I do it myself. I want to have seen everyone, at every level. Afterwards Alain sees them too. Recruitment is something we do very intuitively, not using tests and juries. Everyone who starts here gets opportunities to progress or a chance to go abroad. We do not have training courses, but we do have projects. Every year, for example, we bring together 15 people from different levels and different countries and send them to Alain's workshop in Montpellier for three days. They spend time together there. They eat, drink and talk. There is no agenda. Those people report on their time away when they return to

their own branch and their own colleagues. So it is always a human story.

What is LPQ's philosophy as far as sustainability is concerned?

Whenever we can, we source organic ingredients. This way, we not only build lasting and meaningful partnerships with organic farmers, but we also ensure our ingredients are of the highest quality. It is about finding the very best in a way that is good for all of us. Our philosophy influences every part of the way we do business, from the food we serve to the design of our stores to the materials we use. It is good for our bodies, our communities, and our earth.

In what ways has LPQ already turned its philosophy into practice?

We have implemented sustainable practices, and we keep doing so at different levels of the company. Some practices are global where as others vary in between markets. Worldwide, our furniture is repurposed and/or crafted from reclaimed train floors. We use reclaimed oak for the floor and repurposed architectural salvage for décor. We specify low flow toilets and faucets on all new shops and use VOC paints and recycled gypsum for plaster on the wall. There is LED lighting over the communal table. We use energy star-rated equipment, starch based utensils and PLA cups. We have reusable jute bags for our retail customers. Our entire range of consumer packaged good branded Le Pain Quotidien is organic. We use organic flour (except in two markets: Russia and Switzerland). In some markets our bread is certified organic (e.g. US, UK, France, and Belgium).

Specifically in the United States, Le Pain Quotidien is a Certified Green Restaurant and a member of the Green Restaurant Association. Our field staff wears organic T-shirts. We use environmentally friendly, plant-based cleaning products and hand soap. We recycle and compost at our Support Center. And most of our products and ingredients are organic and certified organic. In the United Kingdom for example, Le Pain Quotidien is a member of the Sustainable Restaurant Association. We source our organic wines and beverages locally. All of our takeaway packaging materials are either compostable or made 100% from recycled products. And finally, we are currently reviewing a proposal to implement a recycling program for 15 locations (out of 20) to achieve sustainable processing and maximum diversion from landfill.

What is the secret of this concept? Why do you think it works everywhere, from Mexico to Dubai?

The secret behind the concept could be its simplicity and its timelessness. The simplicity is reflected in the simple décor, the limited assortment of ingredients and dishes and the minimal communication effort inside or outside our locations.

The secret of its success resides in the continuous effort of the management to stay true to the roots of the concept and its values: conviviality, authenticity, quality, and simplicity. In today's world, it is easy for people to get lost in the overload of information, news and activities surrounding

their daily life. We think that the concept allows guests to slow down, relax and spend time with themselves or family and friends around our communal table which is present in every location worldwide. Another aspect that contributes to the international presence of the concept is that bread, the cornerstone of Le Pain Quotidien's menu, is (in various forms) a staple in many cultures throughout the world.

What is the biggest challenge for LPQ?
The biggest challenge for Le Pain Quotidien is to keep its core values at heart while growing and sharing the concept and lifestyle with more and more people throughout the world.

FABULOUS TO BUY

01. Y water

02. Bee Raw

03. Original Beans

04. Dry Soda

05. BOS Ice Tea

06. Frozen Dutch

07. tap water

08. LunchSkins

09. WB&CO

01
FABULOUS TO BUY

Name **Y water**
URL **ywater.us**
Origin **USA**

organic low-calorie nutrient-rich children's drink

"When it comes to drinking, kids are never taken seriously." In a converted garage on L.A.'s Venice Boulevard, Thomas Arndt explains with unbridled enthusiasm why he started Y water. "If you want to protect your children from all those sugar and colouring-infested soft drinks, there is only one genuine alternative: water. But kids think water is boring which makes it hard to get them to drink enough." Arndt's analysis is very much based on his own experience with raising kids, which lead him to develop Y water: an organic, vitamin-rich and low-calorie soft drink for kids available in four different flavours and packaged in fun, Y-shaped bottles.

How did Y water come about?
At the end of 2005, some time around my 40th birthday, the desire to start my own business grew stronger and stronger. But the big question of course was, "What kind of business?" I am passionate about brands and am deeply inspired by genuine craftsmanship: a good quality boot maker, an old pharmacy, Aqua di Parma, that sort of thing. I looked at existing brands, the ones that already had a certain brand "heritage". But I did not have the money to take over such a company. Around the same time, a friend of mine began working for Capri-sun, the company that sells kid's juices in the famous flexible, silver-coloured bags. He told me that around 5 billion of those bags were sold every year. That inspired me to take a closer look at the soft drinks market for kids. It turned out that there has been hardly any innovation for the past 30 years. The fantastic bottles and other packaging ideas that continue to crop up in the adult drinks sector were virtually unknown in the kids segment. And the health drink trend that played such an important role in my former job also appeared to have flown right past the kids segment. To put it bluntly, all those kids drinks were in fact nothing more than variously flavoured sugar water with lots of calories.

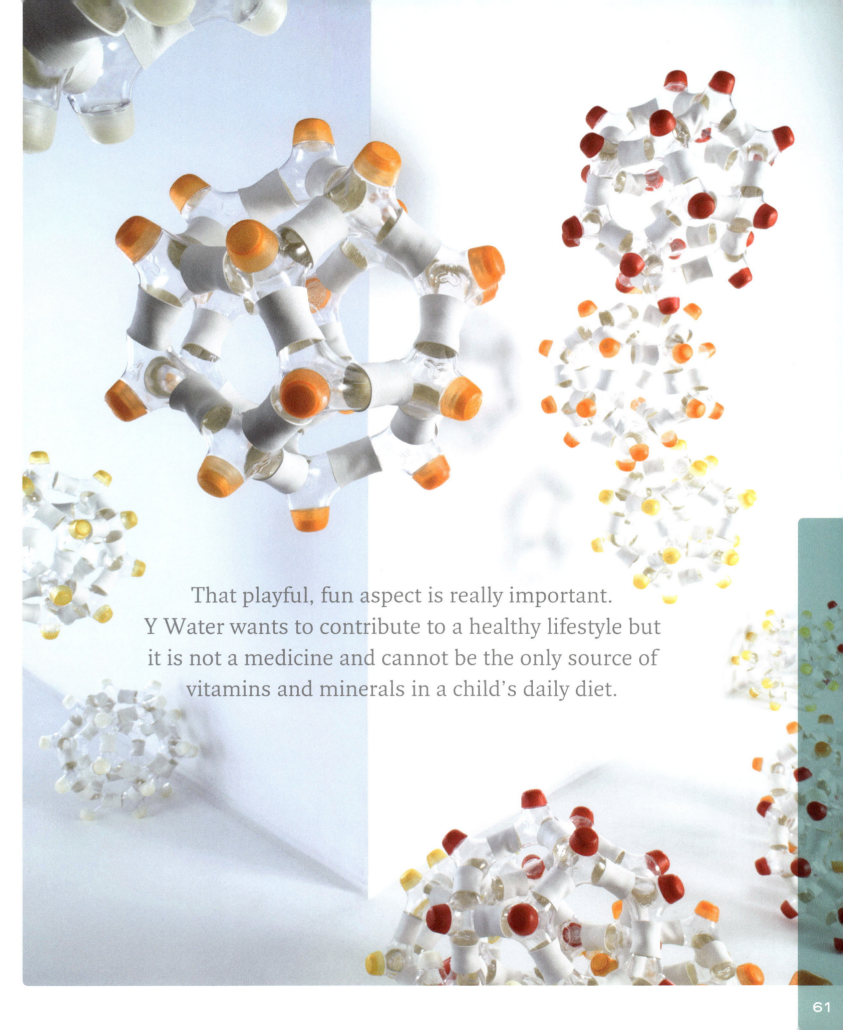

That playful, fun aspect is really important.
Y Water wants to contribute to a healthy lifestyle but it is not a medicine and cannot be the only source of vitamins and minerals in a child's daily diet.

...functional, environmental friendly and made especially for kids.

What did you do before launching Y w ater?

I was the country manager for Carpe Diem Kombucha, a company that launched a line of natural teas on the American market in 2001. Before that I did the same thing in Germany. And before that I worked for the energy drink Red Bull, the mother company of Carpe Diem. I met the owner of Red Bull shortly after finishing my law degree in Frankfurt. At the time, Red Bull was still relatively small and to be honest, I had never even heard of it before. My idea was to have a look for six months or so before starting somewhere else as a lawyer. As it turned out, I ended up staying with the company for 15 years.

What was the conclusion of your study of the kids drinks market?

I had a look around and a think about things and became increasingly convinced that there was room for an alternative. After a year I knew exactly what I wanted:

1. a good product that I could give to my children with a clear conscience
2. an attractive design
3. a green, sustainable formula

I subsequently resigned from my job in 2007 and took the plunge.

How do you go about developing a healthy drink?

I went to the specialists at the Advanced Center for Food Sciences at Cornell University, studied Harvard reviews and hassled paediatricians with a whole host of questions. After some time I had a good idea of what ingredients I wanted in the product. We distinguished four aspects of a child's growth and development which also resulted in the four product names: Muscle Water, Bone Water, Immune Water and Brain Water. At first these were just working titles but we came to like the names more and more as things progressed and we ended up sticking with them. That playful, fun aspect is really important. Y water wants to contribute to a healthy lifestyle but it is not a medicine and cannot be the only source of vitamins and minerals in a child's daily diet. And although it has a lot less calories and sugar than regular kids drinks, it is not 100% (cane) sugar-free. But I would rather give my kids an acceptable level of sweetness as an incentive to drink enough than offer them only water which they do not like.

I then went to a flavour company specialised in organic flavours. At first they came up with the traditional strawberry flavours and so on

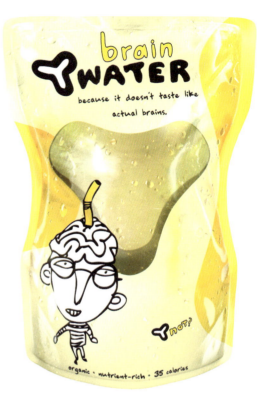

but kids' tastes are often more refined and more imaginative than adults presuppose. In the end, we chose for all sorts of flavours in the water like coriander, caramel, cranberry, lemon, grape, rosemary, and so on. My own kids and their friends have tested it and they loved it. Despite what you think, kids are really quite open to new things.

What is the inspiration behind the packaging?

I wanted something refreshing. Kids have got a real sense for design. Parents think that kids think dinosaurs are the max but they love Nike and iPods even more. I had a shortlist of famous designers like Philippe Starck but also a list of names that were less well known to me but whose work I really liked. At the top of the list was Yves Behar. I called him, he liked the concept and three months later he came and gave a presentation. There were two proposals: a concept with a bag as well as the bottle that we ended up going for. The bottle was inspired by the game of jacks. It also looks a bit like a molecule and has a certain scientific yet playful look about it.

And the name?

The first name we had was Smartkids. We used it for a long time during the development phase but it did not really work. Smartkids is too preachy and kids were never going to use it. "Mum, can you get me another Smartkids from the fridge?" Forget it! Once Yves had presented his jacks concept, the new working name became Jax. And then one day a friend suddenly said, "Why not call it Y? Turn the bottle upside down and you have the letter Y." Plus, aren't kids always asking, "Why?" And then I thought, "Why not?" Since then, our water has been known as Y water.

Our overall objective is to position Y as the first global contemporary lifestyle kids brand.

Y WATER
Nutrition & Hydration for kids

Y WATER is an organic, low calorie, functional drink. It is the first in a new category of "developmental drinks" that provide the vitamins and minerals essential to a child's healthy growth.
Y WATER is available in 4 varieties: muscle water, immune water, bone water and brain water.

Magnesium improves muscle performance. Fruit punch naturally flavored.

Zinc promotes mental performance. Banana pineapple naturally flavored.

Calcium keeps bones and teeth healthy and strong. Orange mango naturally flavored.

Vitamin A, C and E strengthen the immune system. Peach lemonade naturally flavored.

Y WATER is made in the USA under strict quality and safety controls.
The ingredients in Y WATER are recommended by the Institute of Medicine and The American Academy of Pediatrics. Y WATER's manufacturing process was developed by Cornell University to guarantee the highest food quality and ensure maximum food safety.

a new concept in children's beverages

Who did you rely on during the development phase?

I have a small but excellent team of sparring partners. Thomas Grabner is a friend who runs an advertising agency in Santa Monica. I talked to him a lot about Y Water and he gave me a lot of free advice. Yves Behar also had a lot of input, naturally, as did Dietrich Mateschitz, the owner of Red Bull. Dietrich has a very good sense for concepts and the right design. In fact, he has also invested in Y water, as has Yves.

When was Y water launched on the market?

We launched Y water in April 2008 at Whole Foods in California. It was a homerun! The product flew out the shops and was constantly out of stock. We were the best-selling kids drink at Whole Foods. We had to change the business model a bit as we realized that the iconic Y water bottle – with a retail price of $1.99 – was too expensive to be an "everyday beverage", it was more of a "treat". So, we decided to add the Y pouch, a small flexible bag, to our Y water range. With the Y water pouch we can offer the Y water concept – organic, nutrient rich and low calorie – to the mainstream consumer. We are actually very happy with the sales.

Did you have to do a lot of advertising to achieve that?

None at all. We put the water on the shelves and that was all. If you have a product that really makes a difference, people discover it all by themselves. We want to grow organically and give consumers the time to get to know our product. We are also selective in our choice of retailers. And we are investing in a customized production system that will allow us to produce larger volumes. Filling the bottles used to be a pain in the beginning.

Despite what you think, kids are really quite open to new things.

65

Why not call it Y? Turn the bottle upside down and you have the letter Y. Plus, aren't kids always asking, "Why?"

A lot of empty bottles live out a second life as toys.

There was simply no standard filling system that accepted our boomerang-like bottles. In the end we looked at the perfume industry. They also have all kinds of crazy bottles that have to be filled. The solution was to insert our bottles in a second round bottle and thus "trick" the machine into thinking it was a "normal" bottle so it would not go ballistic.

Who is Y water's target group?

In a way we have opened up a premium segment for children's drinks. Y water is relatively expensive compared with other soft drinks. If the volume increases, the price will come down but in the end, we are aiming at responsible parents who are conscious about food and who consider it important that their children eat and drink healthily.

You mentioned a green, sustainable approach. But do you not use a lot of plastic for the bottles?

It is true, we do use quite a lot of plastic. That is because the bottles have to be relatively thick to withstand the high temperatures of sterilization. There is an alternative sterilization method that would allow us to use less thick material but the machine is extremely expensive. At this point we are too small for that. So even though the bottles are 100% recyclable, our footprint is still larger than we are comfortable with. Nevertheless, we are doing all we can to reduce it. For example, we have the Y to Y programme where you can send your bottle back to us free of charge. We make sure the bottles are reused. And we are currently working on a dishwasher safe, reusable Y

water bottle. A lot of empty bottles, however, live out a second life as toys. We developed special "Y knots" that let kids make all kinds of figures by joining the bottles together. The Y pouch is a flexible packaging which makes it superior to any rigid packaging, from an environmental point of view. The actual content is 100% "green". The ingredients and the filling process are organic and we do not use artificial colourings.

What is your vision on the future for Y water?

We want to constantly prove our innovative capabilities and optimize our current packaging and product. Our overall objective is to position Y as the first global contemporary lifestyle kids brand. We have several product ideas that could be launched under the Y label, but there is no hurry. Think of Y toothpaste, Y sports wear etc.... - all functional, environmental friendly and made especially for kids. However, the important thing is that if you launch something, it has to be good right from the start. You only ever get one chance to do things properly.

As far as distribution is concerned, as I have said already, our buyers are responsible parents. There are responsible parents all over the world, so in that sense Y Water is a global concept that could work just as well in L.A. as Frankfurt or Tokyo. At this point we are focusing on Los Angeles and New York. In most premium and natural retailers you can find our range. But we are exploring the international market and we are very excited at the prospect of distributing Y water in Hong Kong and soon Switzerland.

02 FABULOUS TO BUY

Name **Bee Raw Honey**
URL **beeraw.com**
Origin **USA**

100% raw varietal honey

Zeke Freeman was a buyer at Dean&Deluca when he was contacted by Anne Beckers in the late 1990s. "I want to do something with honey", she said. Anne had contacts with beekeepers and she showed him some test-tubes of honey. Zeke looked carefully at her story, found it interesting and became a consultant to Anne's new company Beehive Bee Products, which later became Bee Raw Honey. Zeke: When Anne contacted me, D&D was only selling imported honey from France, Greece and Italy – nothing from the US. There was not a single attractive brand, just small-scale beekeepers working alone.

How did your consultancy work begin?

Anne had a great product and we set out to make some suitable packaging. The vials needed to show off the beauty of the honey. The reasoning behind this was that the product should speak for itself. So there was little or no information, we just showed off what was in the vial. I was the first customer and soon there were more. Anne was an artist and after a while the business side of it became too much for her. Since I had known the business from the beginning, I decided to take over the company.

Where does the honey come from?

We only work with beekeepers who produce honey from wild floral sources or organic floral sources. Reducing the exposure of

We buy the honey from small American beekeepers who like to make healthy honey insecticides. We visit the beekeepers to see where the hives are located and what crops are grown in the immediate vicinity. If insecticides are used in the immediate area it is of course likely that the bees will take it up and the insecticides will find their way into the honey. That is not what we want. To avoid this we look for hives that are located near organically grown crops or wild flora.

So is the honey organic?
Under American legislation you can only call the honey organic if there is no agriculture within 40 square miles of the beehive. That is virtually impossible in the US, so officially certified organic honey is not made anywhere in America. However, by being aware of this and using common sense, you can prevent harmful insecticides finding their way into the honey.

After a time the name was changed to Bee Raw Honey.
Because it's a call to action—it's a call to purity. Our honey is raw, which means unprocessed. Most of the honey you find in supermarkets is processed. It has been heated to 180 degrees and passed through very fine filters. That filters the pollen and a number of other ingredients out of the honey. The industry labels these ingredients as harmful, but we call them flavour. If you take those out the honey crystallises more slowly and it retains its amber-brown colour for a very long time. American consumers have been told for years that crystallisation is bad.

> We look for hives that are located near organically grown crops or wild flora.

We want to re-educate those consumers: a honey that crystallises is a honey with a better, purer taste.

Do you work with American beekeepers?

When Anne started out she had some French and Australian honey. However, we soon realised how difficult the situation was for American beekeepers. They had already been hit by the imported mites that had killed large numbers of wild bees. In addition, 80 to 85% of the honey in the American market comes from China and Argentina. This honey is dumped at very low prices, making it difficult for American beekeepers to earn a living. So we are not only concerned about quality and aesthetics. Helping American beekeepers is definitely another core value for us.

If the demand increases, will you still be able to work with just small-scale beekeepers?

Certainly. The last thing we want is for beekeepers to evolve into industrial businesses because of increasing demand. Instead we want to get to know their neighbours, and then their neighbours' neighbours, so that our network of small, family-run beekeepers can continue to grow.

The word-of-mouth effect plays an important part in this. The beekeeper community is a small community in which everyone knows everyone else. In the beginning we were working with two or three beekeepers, and now we work with about ten.

How many different varietals are there?
There are nine different varietals available all year round. There are another three or four varietals which are only available in smaller quantities during specific seasons. As well as individual honeys we have also created a number of gift sets, consisting of four to nine different varietals mounted in a block of oak.

Is the price of a jar of Bee Raw Honey much higher than other honeys?
It certainly is. A jar of Bee Raw Honey costs 9.99 USD, while a similar quantity of processed honey costs 5.99 USD on average. There are a number of reasons for this. We pay our beekeepers a premium price for a premium product. The packaging is not cheap either. We do not stick labels onto our glass jars; the letters are engraved in the glass. This is more environmentally friendly, but also a more complex process.

Who do you sell to?
We sell to retailers who make a point of offering real food. These include stores such as Dean&Deluca and Wholefoods. We have also exported some honey, but we are quite cautious about this. Our main aim is not to grow as fast as possible, but rather to be and

We want to re-educate those consumers: a honey that crystallises is a honey with a better, purer taste.

Helping American beekeepers is definitely another core value for us.

Our main aim is not to grow as fast as possible, but rather to be and remain a sustainable business.

remain a sustainable business. If you start exporting, that means that someone else is opening up a new market with your product. So you definitely need to be on the same wavelength as that person or business.

Do you advertise?

No, never. We do a lot of PR though. My wife has worked in advertising for 20 years and the wife of my business partner Sam Yocum has her own PR agency. So we have a large network of publishers, journalists and writers. Of course we would never try to push anything onto them. We just say: "Take a look".

I do put a lot of time and energy into our retailers and distributors. Day-to-day sales are outsourced but I visit a lot of stores and distributors to tell them the story behind the product. In that sense education is really at the heart of our marketing effort. Stores always ask for free products or discounts, but I offer them training courses instead. I tell them about honey production and American beekeepers. I give them recipes, describe the cocktails you can make using honey and tell them which cheeses go with which types of honey. The result of this is that staff in the stores become enthusiastic about the product so that they can then sell it effectively.

How do you see the business evolving?

There are still a lot of opportunities for growth in our market. We supply no more than 20 to 25% of high-end grocery stores in the US. Our products are also perfectly suited for use as gifts, but we have not even started on that sector yet. And then there is export. As I have said we are cautious about this, but sooner or later it will happen. So there are plenty of opportunities for growth, although growing rapidly is not really our main aim. At present I am the only person working full-time for Bee Raw Honey. I do of course provide work for a number of people, but they are not employees. That is a very comfortable situation, and I would like to keep it that way.

03 FABULOUS TO BUY

Name Original Beans
URL originalbeans.com
Origin The Netherlands

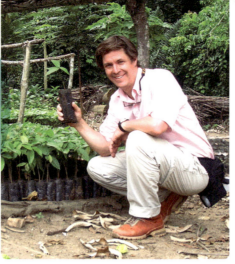

chocolate and rainforest conservation

Original Beans co-founder and conservation entrepreneur Philipp Kauffmann has sustainability running through his veins. In 1791 his direct forefather, Georg Ludwig Hartig, already pointed out in his thesis that "'any wise forest management must use the forest in such a way that generations thereafter can draw at least as much advantage from it as the presently living generation." For Kauffmann nature conservation is the biggest challenge facing us and future generations. "Original beans is founded on the simple idea that what we consume we must replenish."

Chocolate is made from cacao and cacao trees grow in rainforests. It is simple, one cannot exist without the other. And 'we' cannot exist without the rainforest. And yet the mainstream cacao industry keeps on plundering. Kauffmann is very clear about it: "If we wish to continue consuming, then together we must find ways to conserve and replenish the bounty of the Earth." That is why Originals Beans was founded. When Kauffmann met a Dutch fair trade pioneer and an American organic food marketer in 2006, they decided to create a sustainable chocolate that would help restore the rainforest.

By subsidising and educating local farmer communities Original Beans teaches them how to grow cacao without destroying the forests. Reforestation is their remedy. "Active replanting is the best buffer to protect old, primary rainforests." For each bar you buy local farmers plant one tree in the forest of origin. Inside every bar there is a tracking number leading back to the rainforest where the new tree will be planted. The farmers do not just plant cacao trees, but also other trees that are necessary to preserve biodiversity.

According to Kauffmann we have to adjust our perception of chocolate and focus on quality rather than quantity. "The flavour of the bar is most heavily influenced by what happens at the forest level. It is determined by the health of the trees and the farmers' skills in pruning, harvesting, fermenting and drying the beans. Each regional chocolate, like a fine wine, is a reflection of the local "terroir".

Originals Beans comes in four flavours:

Piura Porcelana from Peru:
'porcelana' is the forgotten white cacao variety that was nearly extinct. In 2006 it was rediscovered in the foothills of the Andes and brought back into production. The Original Beans' replanting programme enabled local farmers to go from rice to cacao. Result: the farmer has a higher income and it is better for nature. *Tasting notes: vibrant, luscious with kumquat, lime, apricot, raspberry flavours and notes of toasted pecan; wonderfully balanced acidity and lingering finish.*

Cru Virunga from Eastern Congo:
'cru virunga' is the first single-origin cacao variety grown in Virunga National Park, Africa's oldest nature reserve and home to the last mountain gorillas on earth. Original Beans built nurseries, introduced training programmes for local farmer communities and started replanting the forest to help protect and rebuild a region that was recovering from war.
Tasting notes: zingy with ripe morello cherries, steeped in cassis, smokey tobacco and forest floor notes; great smoothness, length and nuance.

Beni Wild harvest from Bolivia:
'beni wild' is 100% wild cacao from Bolivia which grows on "chocolatales" or "cacao islands". During the wet season experts from indigenous tribes go out in canoes to collect the wild beans. Original Beans is actively involved in the conservation of this rare cacao variety.
Tasting notes: sun-dried cranberries, melon, subtle tropical fruit notes, hints of jasmine tea;

Original beans is founded on the simple idea that what we consume we must replenish

delicate yet distinct, wonderfully round flavour and long finish.

Esmeraldas Milk from Ecuador: with the help of small producer cooperatives in the Esmeraldas region Original Beans aims to conserve the threatened 'arriba' variety and protect the rainforests in which it grows.

Tasting notes: salted caramel, honey, hints of summer red fruits and spice; exceptional velvety smoothness and mouth-filling finish.

04
FABULOUS TO BUY

Name Dry Soda
URL drysoda.com
Origin USA

all natural soda

Sharelle Klaus and her husband enjoy good food with a glass of fine wine. During her four pregnancies, however, she was forced to leave out the wine and found the alternatives that were offered rather uninspiring. This observation led to the creation of DRY Soda. The interview with DRY's marketing manager BreeAnna Marchitto took place at the company's Tasting Room in the heart of Seattle.

How exactly did DRY come into being?

BreeAnna (marketing manager): After giving birth to her fourth child, Sharelle Klaus wanted to create a beverage that would serve as a replacement for wine in restaurants. The various juices and sodas that she was offered during her pregnancy were usually far too sweet and overwhelmed the taste of the food. Sharelle's beverage not only had to taste good; it had to be healthy, less sweet and natural. In 2005 she set to work in her own kitchen. She read everything she could find about creating beverages, researched dozens of flavour profiles and asked for help from local chefs. Sharelle cherished positive memories of many different flavours. Lavender reminded her of her garden, while rhubarb reminded her of grandmother's rhubarb pies . She did a lot of research, boiled up basic ingredients to obtain extracts and bought a CO_2 home carbonator. She made one test drink after another and gave them to her family to taste. In August 2005 all this research resulted in the first four DRY flavours: Lavender, Kumquat, Lemongrass and Rhubarb.

Have more flavours arrived since those early days?

Yes, more than two years after the launch we asked Jason Wilson, the chef and owner of the famous Crush restaurant in Seattle to help create a few new flavours. Jason was very enthusiastic and ultimately came up with 12 different options. We took the team to his restaurant to taste them, and finally we came away with Juniper Berry and Vanilla

During her four pregnancies, Sharelle was forced to leave out the wine and found the alternatives that were offered rather uninspiring.

Bean. In 2009 we added Cucumber DRY, and in 2010 we replaced Kumquat DRY with Blood Orange DRY and just launched Wild Lime for a total line of eight flavours.

Why the name DRY?

The word 'dry' is used to refer to wines that are not sweet, and that is true of DRY Soda too. The word DRY also arouses curiosity when it is used to describe a drink.

Why is DRY healthy?

This beverage contains only four natural ingredients and it is not packed with lots of unknown additives. First of all you have purified carbonated water. Next come the natural flavour extracts, which are organic in most cases. The third ingredient is pure cane sugar, with only a small quantity being added (14-19 grammes per bottle). Finally, phosphorus, a natural mineral, is the only preservative used.

Each bottle contains between 45 and 70 calories, while a traditional soft drink can easily pack in 150 to 180 calories.

How sustainable is DRY?

The bottles that we use are recyclable and the caps biodegradable, and we use as many local and organic ingredients as possible.

To my mind, however, the most sustainable aspect is the fact that we are marketing a natural soda containing just four ingredients which has an attractive flavour and minimal sugar content and which is much healthier than most of the alternatives.

Where is DRY sold?

In 2005 Sharelle began with the top 30 restaurants in Seattle. She presented DRY to them, and all 30 chefs were enthusiastic and added DRY to their menus. More and more restaurants then joined this customer base, many of them outside Seattle, and DRY is now available in restaurants nationwide. Later on the retail market was approached as well. Today DRY is available throughout the US from many retailers such as Whole Foods, Kroger and Dean & Deluca.

Who came up with the design?

Seattle-based Turnstyle Studio is responsible for all the artwork, the logo, packaging materials, the website, etc. When designing the bottles it was important to express the purity of the product, hence the transparent glass bottles. Each bottle also bears Sharelle's signature to express her personal involvement in creating and choosing the flavours.

Looking to the future, we would like to establish DRY as a new category of sodas, less sweet, all natural, and better for you.

Do you advertise?

No, so far we have not spent a single dollar on advertising, instead we focus on more grassroots effort such as social media and events. Our presence at all kinds of food, wine and celebrity events allows people to try DRY for themselves. We opened our tasting-room here in Seattle with the same aim in mind. You can taste all our flavours here, and the room is also available for hire if you wish to organise a private event. We have found that social media sites such as Facebook and Twitter have really allowed us to communicate and interact directly with current and potential customers of DRY. They have been invaluable in DRY's growth and name-brand recognition.

What is the big goal?

Looking to the future, we would like to establish DRY as a new category of sodas, less sweet, all natural, and better for you. We also plan to launch additional original flavours to the DRY line.

In addition, it would be great if DRY could be available outside North America. We are already selling to Hong Kong and we have some contacts in Korea. To realise these international ambitions, the most important thing is working with the right exporters and importers, people who can work with DRY and share our vision about the future of beverages.

05
FABULOUS TO BUY

Name **BOS Ice Tea**
URL **bosicetea.com**
Origin **South Africa**

organic rooibos ice tea blended with natural flavours

BOS is a fairly new South African organic ice tea brand launched in July 2010. The name BOS comes from the South African slang word "bossies", meaning 'bushes that grow in dry and arid regions'. 'Bossi-estee' is rooibos tea, which brings us to the primary ingredient of all BOS ice tea: first grade organic rooibos, an indigenous South African product that is unique to the Western Cape's Cederberg region. Blended with natural fruit flavours and ancient beneficial ingredients, it makes for a healthy alternative to regular soft drinks.

For every 2000 cans of BOS ice tea sold, a tree is planted and maintained in underprivileged areas with little green in South Africa. So, when you are drinking BOS ice tea, you can be proud of yourself as

BOS /bos/ noun, adj & verb. -n.

1. deliciously refreshing ice tea made entirely in South Africa with enormous integrity and care.
2. a cool tea with a cool taste in a cool can.

-adj. 1. possessing out the box originality, unleashed energy, robust health and an exuberant capacity for joy.
2. wildly inspired.
3. typically presented in Afro pop packaging.

colloq. mad. outrageous. rooibos – **verb intr.** go bos.
– **verb tr.** bossificate (as in to Bossify, to be converted to BOS, or to subscribe to the BOS way of life).

well, because you are helping reduce the global impact of climate change.

The BOS brand, packaging and ice teas were conceived by founder and brand expert Grant Rushmere, who developed an international coffee and tea brand called Afro. When he was working on Afro, he experimented a lot with Rooibos, blending it with all kinds of flavours. That is how he discovered it would make a perfect base for ice tea. The natural sweetness of rooibos makes it the ideal carrier for fruit flavours, and in addition to that rooibos is known for its healing qualities due to a high level of anti-oxidants. In 2009, Rushmere partnered up with Richard Bowsher, organic rooibos farmer and entrepreneur. They shared a dream: to start an ethically managed business, from farm to

> It is a beautiful, extremely biodiverse piece of land situated in the Western Cape's Cederberg mountains. They call it BOS country.

table, one that would also build awareness around African products. Together they launched BOS ice teas into the South African market in July 2010 from their headquarters in Woodstock, Cape Town.

The organic rooibos, core ingredient of all BOS ice teas, is grown at the Klipopmekaar Rooibos Tea Farm and Private Nature Reserve (www.klipopmekaar.co.za), owned by BOS co-founder Richard Browsher. It is a beautiful, extremely biodiverse piece of land situated in the Western Cape's Cederberg mountains. They call it BOS country. Klipopmekaar is committed to producing in an ethical, environmentally sustainable and socially responsible way. The use of solar energy, organic farming methods, environmentally conscious design, recycling systems, projects to preserve biodiversity and the respect for the farmers who work the land illustrate their beliefs. Only 10% of Klipopmekaar is farmed, the other 90% (over 4,500 hectares) is mountain wilderness.

BOS Ice tea comes in 5 flavours. Three in the classic range including Lemon, Peach and Apple. The other two in the Utility range: BOS Slim, lime & ginger flavoured,

and BOS Energy, lightly sparkling cranberry flavoured, to which a touch of naturally beneficial ingredients is added, like hoodia gordonii (to suppress appetite) and guarana (energy booster). The colourful African pop art can was designed to express the purity, energy and carefree spirit of the brand. The use of strong African symbols like the lion and Sirius, the brightest star promising sustenance, wellbeing and abundance, are a reference to ancient African mythology. BOS aims to be a young, contemporay, stylish brand, yet firmly rooted in African culture.

When asked why he chose to create an ice tea, Rushmere explains: "The South African ice tea market is relatively small compared to international markets. Globally, the ice tea market is one of the fastest growing segments within the soft drink market. As choices shift to healthier options, ice tea finds itself as the perfect offering. And because it is a drink that has not nearly been harnessed to its full potential. An ice tea could have it all – entertainment, refreshment, health...and a conscience. BOS is not just an ice tea, it is also an experience and a way of looking at life."

06 FABULOUS TO BUY

Name Frozen Dutch
URL frozendutch.nl
Origin The Netherlands

organic ice cream following the seasons

Amsterdam ice-cream producers Reint Jan Schuring and Reggy Gunn started their adventure in 2009 as complete novices, but they could not be deterred from realising their shared ambition. Frozen Dutch is their response to the decline of traditional ice cream making in the Netherlands.

At Frozen Dutch the emphasis is on seasonal organic fruit and vegetable ice creams using locally sourced ingredients. Flavour is their trademark. "To bring out the flavour of the fruit even more than when you eat the fruit itself, that is the art of making ice cream", says Schuring.

Reint Jan Schuring first trained as a sociologist, but as it turned out that was not his calling. After several years in the advertising sector he decided it was time to really make something, and what he made was traditional ice cream. "Dutch ice cream truly is trending towards zero. Two litres are now sold for 1.29 euro. Soon they will be giving you money to take away a litre of ice cream. That says something about what is in it." According to Reint, ice cream must above all be delicious. He is convinced that consumers are willing to pay a little more for that. Co-founder Reggy Gunn is not only a visual artist, but a teacher and an enthusiastic cook as well. His feeling for materials and flavours fits in perfectly at Frozen Dutch. "It is a wonderful thing to work on a great product and also to try and create a brand and express a philosophy. Even the name makes it clear that Frozen Dutch is exactly that. Our approach is to use local fruit and vegetables wherever possible. That is sustainable by definition. It is all about flavour, quality, sustainability and being organic."

Flavour always comes first. The two ice-cream makers strive to create strong, pure flavours, and have no interest at all in complex mixtures of unnecessary ingredients. That is why they prefer real vanilla pods which leave small black dots in the ice cream or use up to 16 large cucumbers for one tub of cucumber-dill sorbet. All the ingredients are organic and the product contains a minimum of 50% fresh fruit or vegetables, while the flavours follow the seasons; rhubarb-ginger in spring, red currant-vanilla in summer, followed by star anise-pear and apple-cinnamon later in the year.

The seasonal range consists mainly of sorbets with no milk at all, only water, fruit and in some cases added sugars, but they also make traditional ice cream in basic flavours like vanilla, chocolate and coffee. A third product is the sherbet, a combination of sorbet and ice cream, and finally there

is frozen yoghurt, based on yoghurt, fruit, water and sugar. Frozen Dutch was awarded the Eko label in March 2011, which means it is now officially recognised as an organic product.

Schuring and Gunn supply organic supermarkets, caterers and restaurants. In the future they intend to expand their production capacity and are hoping to work directly with growers so that they can follow the seasons even more closely.

07
FABULOUS TO BUY

Name **tap water™**
URL **tapwater-bottle.com**
Origin **Canada**

refillable glass water bottle

According to Racquel Youtzy, Toronto-based founder of the tap water™ bottle, drinking water in plastic bottles is a choice, not a necessity. There may have been times when people believed bottled water was healthier, today we know it is not. In addition, the impact of bottled water on the environment is enormous. With less than 20% recycled, most plastic bottles end up in landfills or even worse, on beaches or in oceans where it takes over a thousand years to break down. Excessive amounts of energy and water are needed to produce them, and then there is the transport. "If plastic bottles got frequent flyer miles, they'd be traveling business class for free, forever." Racquel's concern for the environment goes back a long way, but she actually wanted to contribute. In 2009, she launched her tap water™ bottle, because she is convinced that the most effective way to reduce our global carbon footprint is to focus on re-use.

The tap water™ bottle is a reusable glass water bottle that comes in three sizes. The design of the bottle is simple, stylish and clean, the perfect carrier for tap water.
On each bottle a message is printed, so the user will not forget why plastic bottles are wrong.

Re-use is the most significant environmental impact we can make.

250ml - They say the best things in life are free. Really? Water is right at the top of that list and these days a bottle of water costs more per litre than gasoline. That's about as far from free as it gets. Tap water on the other hand is totally free. Just turn on any old tap and you'll get water that, in most cases, is better regulated and certainly cheaper than water that comes in a plastic bottle. So maybe the best things in life are free. And refillable ;)

500ml - Life is full of choices: big and small. Sometimes a small choice like choosing to buy bottled water over drinking tap water, casts a big shadow. Making this small choice means you're supporting an industry that ships billions of tiny bottles of water overseas, often taking it from people who lack access to clean drinking water and selling it to people with so much of it they flush it away. Hmmm. Small choice?

1 litre - In the good old days, mineral water and spring water didn't come in the "convenient" plastic bottles they do today. Bottles which, after a single use, find their way to our oceans breaking down into millions of pieces. These pieces are gobbled up by marine animals which are then eaten by other animals and so on until eventually those bottles end up in the food on our plates. So next time you pass up on tap water for that "healthier" option, do us all a favour, eat the bottle too.

How did you come up with the idea?

I felt inspired to create the tap water™ bottle after seeing awful sights of plastic water bottle garbage and learning of the horrible effects it has on the planet. As I learnt more I felt further and further inspired. It is simply a healthier choice for our bodies and our environments. As the popularity of bottled water is mainly due to its convenience, I wanted to make a product that was still portable and visually appealing enough to help provide inspiration to make a smarter choice. Glass is one of the oldest and most trusted methods for packaging liquids. It is made from naturally occurring minerals and does not carry health risks, related to toxic chemicals leaching from plastic containers. Glass is the best vessel for beverages, and it looks good. The difficulty was finding a bottle that had all the elements of style, design and durability that I wished for. It took just over a year to complete the final product with the first message on the bottle. And as every new print will have a new message for the world, to help inspire and educate, I hope there will be many more.

Does it not break easily?

The glass tap water™ bottle is not unbreakable. You need to be careful with it, just as you need to be careful with your health and the environment.

Why is tap water healthier? Is the quality better than the quality of bottled water?

This is a big YES and there are SO many reasons why. For example, tap water is always moving, that way it stays fresh. It is filtered, disinfected and in most countries it is far better regulated and undergoes more frequent testing, usually many times a day. It is hard to image that bottled water that is less regulated and sometimes exposed to high temperatures when stored can be purer than tap water. When water is stored in plastic containers, it takes on some of the chemicals the plastic is made from.

What is the philosophy behind the tap water™ bottle?

Re-use is the most significant environmental impact we can make. Despite our best efforts, the vast majority of plastic water bottles are not recycled. Even if recycling were to approach 100 percent, it is not a perfect process. It requires energy and creates additional waste. If every one person tries, with just a little bit of effort, we can make a difference - beautifully.

How big is the impact of bottled water on the environment?

Bottled water is a waste of our natural resources. Transporting bottled water burns massive quantities of fossil fuels. Fossil fuels are also used in the packaging of the water. Then crude oil is wasted in making the plastic for the bottles. Which when producing requires water - it can take up to five litres of water to make just one litre of bottled water. The whole process results in over half a dozen air pollutants. On top of that, less than 20% is recycled. Unlike bottled water our bottles only make the trip once, while empty, and are to be RE-used FOREVER.

Which arguments would you use to convince people to buy a tap water™ bottle?

It is just such a simple choice that is better for your health, your world and your wallet. Bottled water is ridiculously expensive and in some cases, what you are buying is actually tap water.

What is your ultimate goal?

To see an end to the indulgence of bottled water. The plastic water bottle has become a symbol of our disposable culture at its most thoughtless. It is a luxury we afford ourselves that is wasteful of our water, when more than one out of six people in the world lack access to safe drinking water.

If plastic bottles got frequent flyer miles, they'd be traveling business class for free, forever.

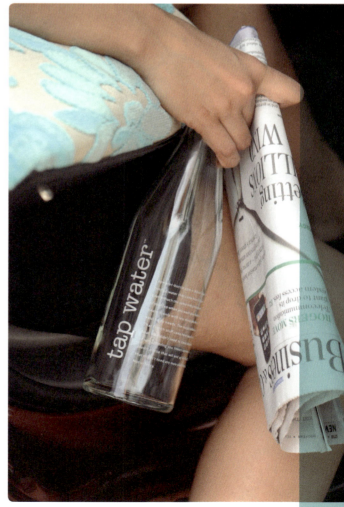

08
FABULOUS TO BUY

Name **LunchSkins**
URL **lunchskins.com**
Origin **USA**

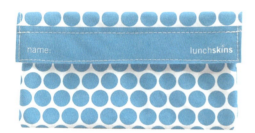

Lunchskins are a green product because they can be reused multiple times and they make a disposable product, the plastic lunch bag, superfluous.

eco-friendly alternative to the plastic lunch bag

We do not think about it very often - one plastic bag more or less does not seem to make much of a difference. However, if you consider that 20 million plastic lunch bags are dumped in landfill in the US every day, and only 1-3% of these are actually recycled, that one bag becomes more significant.

For Kirsten Quigley, Cristina Bourelly and Jennie Stoller Barakat, facing up to these alarming facts spurred them to join forces in the battle against plastic. They became the 3GreenMoms, with a single green mission: to come up with an environmentally friendly alternative to the old-fashioned, polluting plastic lunch bag. Under the motto "reduce your daily lunchprint" they have brought Lunch-Skins to the market.

Since plastic bags are not biodegradable and consequently do not completely disappear, they represent a major threat to both land and sea. Natural resources such as water and oil are also plundered to produce the quantities that we "need" today. Although it may have been an innovative invention 40 years ago, the plastic bag is now completely outmoded. The 3GreenMoms thought it was high time to come up with an alternative. These ladies had always been very focused on nature and outdoor living, and they want more than anything to create a secure future for their children. LunchSkins was the result of their belief that small initiatives can make a difference. "If everyone lives a more sustainable everyday life, that will have a major impact on the health of our planet."

There were several obstacles to overcome, since the LunchSkins had to meet a number of conditions. They had to be environmentally friendly, reusable, dishwasher proof, food-safe, stylish and practical.

They began by searching for materials that are suitable for packaging food and strong

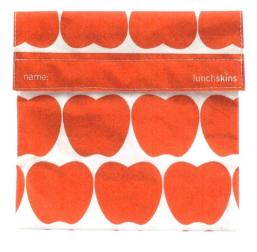

> If everyone lives a more sustainable everyday life, that will have a major impact on the health of our planet.

enough to cope with numerous trips through the dishwasher or washing machine. The 3GreenMoms very soon found themselves talking to the food industry. After some in-depth research they found a very robust variety of cotton that is used in bakeries and restaurants in Europe. It is heatproof and impermeable to grease and moisture, like a bag for piping whipped cream. A wafer-thin layer of polyurethane is applied to the inside. This has no harmful health effects, as confirmed by testing. Although the material comes from Europe, LunchSkins are printed in-house and hand-sewn by a family business in the area. They are available in three sizes: the snack bag (small), the sandwich bag (medium), and the sub bag (large).

To translate their idea into an attractive product, they brought in creative director and GreenMom Jennie Stoller Barakat, who produced some stylish prints in striking colours. LunchSkins are a green product because they can be reused multiple times and they make a disposable product, the plastic lunch bag, superfluous. The result is less pollution and a smaller waste mountain. The efforts made by the 3GreenMoms to reduce their ecological footprint have also gone beyond LunchSkins. As a company they use almost no paper (everything is done online), packaging is reduced to a minimum and made of recycled materials, promotional materials are printed by a local printer on recycled paper, and they cycle to and from work.

The story of Lunchskins began in 2008 with a small green idea. In 2010 Lunchskins succeeded in reducing the size of the waste mountain by 120 million plastic lunch bags. This is only a start, but it is already clear that their mission has been more than successful.

09
FABULOUS TO BUY

Name WB&CO
URL   wbcouk.com
Origin United Kingdom

100% pure juice from organic locally-grown vegetables

For WB&CO, the biggest challenge facing the food industry is food waste.

Much sooner than planned Mark Walker hit Wallpaper Magazine with his brand new vegetable juice brand Wild Bunch Juices, and business broke loose. Two years before, while working in the advertising industry in London and New York, Mark suffered from a medical condition, which meant he had to change his diet. "Nothing serious but I was obliged to make certain adjustments. One was that I could no longer drink fruit juice because it has too much natural sugar. Therefore I had to switch to vegetable juice and I soon discovered that unfortunately there was not so much choice available for vegetable juice as there was for fruit juice."

He researched the best way to make vegetable juice, detected some old European techniques and developed a machine to make beetroot and carrot juice, for himself and his partner. He was quite happy with the results but never intended to market it.

However, he did not count on the word-of-mouth promotion that got into its stride. Before he knew he was delivering pure organic cold-pressed vegetable juices not only to family but also to friends, and friends of friends.

Mid 2007 Mark launched Wild Bunch Juices in Singapore. Because of ambitious plans to

make more vegetable products, the name was gradually re-baptized into WB&CO or Wild Bunch & Co. Soups, biscuits and even vegetable skin care products are on the programme. In 2010, Wild Bunch&Co entered the UK market. The line is currently sold at Waitrose, Daylesford Organic, Selfridges and other "leading" retailers.

Can you tell me more about how things went concretely from production for personal use to business?

"Some time after I started making the juices for myself, my mother-in-law got cancer. She recovered, but while she was in remission she was too weak to eat. Her body could not digest food so she could not take in the energy and nutrients she needed. Therefore I began making vegetable juice for her. It did her well. She told her doctor about it, he told other patients and soon we began receiving requests from diabetics, people with cancer and people on restricted diets. In the beginning it was kindness among friends but after a while the urge to deal with it more properly grew. Our first mission was how to help people on restricted diets to get stronger. And then it grew from there to targeting other people as well, people who want to live a healthy live. That became our second and off course main customer group."

> Sustainable initiatives are never the product of one company, if retailers did not make the effort to collect the glass bottles these ideas would never work.

Can people get cured when they drink the juices?

"No, I do want to stress that this is a complementary therapy. We are not going around telling people it is a treatment or a cure. But as everybody knows, eating or drinking vegetables does help a big deal to build resistance. Plenty of raw fresh organic vegetables in your diet are an insurance policy that can guard against future diseases, as the vitamins, minerals and phytonutrients speed up the action of the body's natural detoxification process. That is the whole genesis of the company: it began from providing people the nutritional benefits of organic vegetable juice. The reason why that is important today is because it is still part of our business. It also means that everything we make is completely natural because cancer patients cannot take any toxins into their bodies so there are no additives, no pasteurization and no preservatives. Other vegetable juice brands can sit on the shelf for more than a year. WB&Co is absolutely pure organic juice."

The name speaks for itself. Why did you change it into WB&CO?

"The idea for the name came from us. We did not go through large brainstorms, it was a simple process. It is a simple and fun name, not abstract. It is organic so it is wild. The name connects with people easily, also with those on a restricted diet. When people are ill they do not want to be reminded of that and they certainly do not want to be approached with more Latin names.

We changed the name of our company to WB&CO because of two different reasons: we want to provide our customers with new vegetable products, other than juice, and we were also planning to go oversees so we needed an even more international name."

What is the company mission today?

"Offer vegetable products in exciting and innovative ways. Vegetables are not appreciated the way they should. We want to make the use of vegetables more convenient so it becomes part of people's daily lives. We are what we eat. But people need to accept that concept and then they will realize that vegetables are an important part of the quality of your life."

Can you tell me more about the production of the juices?

"We daily produce pure organic cold-pressed vegetable Juice. Each morning, the juice goes from our WB&CO Pressing Plant in London straight into the stores. The juice is a hundred percent organic. The organic veggies and herbs we use are sourced locally and are certified as organic at source. Our current range includes Organic Carrot & Ginger, Organic Beetroot, Carrot & Celery and Organic Spinach, Carrot & Parsley. The absolute profit with organic vegetables is that they can contain up to forty percent more vitamins and minerals than non-organic and that they are naturally sweet to taste as they contain less water."

You first opened a WB&CO shop in Singapore while you were living in England. Why Singapore?

"We indeed launched the Wild Bunch shop bar in Singapore, just to put the product down to market. We had an idea but there was no real business model. To a degree it was uncharted territory and that is why we started in Singapore. A good thing about Singapore is that it is small and ideal to test a new product, to see what people buy and what they reject. In Singapore, you get a sample of what may happen somewhere else because it consists of such a cross section of people. Soon after the shop was opened, Wallpaper ran an article on us and we got an awful lot of response. We actually did not plan that because we were in a stage where we still wanted to learn before sending out press releases or hyping the brand up. Business boomed faster than we planned."

Other vegetable juice brands can sit on the shelf for more than a year. WB&Co is absolutely pure organic juice."

We are what we eat. But people need to accept that concept and then they will realize that vegetables are an important part of the quality of your life.

The WB&CO bottles are like little design pieces. Who took care of the design?

"One thing I knew for sure: I did not want dancing or jumping carrots on the bottles. The bottles had to be simple, beautiful and stylish but most of all different than other brands in that category. So we searched for inspiration in another sector: the one of cosmetics and more specifically perfumes. That is where the shape of the bottle comes from. It is quite organic and it has balance. It is really all about communicating the respect for the product and the concept. The design is a perfect reflection of our quality. Seed Singapore designed the logo and the bottle.

Do you spend a lot on marketing and communications?

"Our product range is not mainstream. When we are talking to our customers who have severe illnesses there are even restrictions to what we can say. So we do not actively target those people. We mainly reach them through word-of-mouth and when we talk at conferences. It is a very distinct market and will represent in the long term probably no more than 10% of our business.

With the second customer group, the majority, we can communicate through our retail channels. We work with stores who cater to our customers. To this end much of our advertising and promotion is driven by in-store marketing.

WB&CO is organic but are you all the way green?

In my opinion no company who manufactures and distributes on any reasonable scale can claim to be, "all the way green". Like many companies, we work within the waste management infrastructure of the local authority (in our case London) and try to combine this with our company's own initiatives. In regards to these initiatives, we refill and reuse approximately 30% of our glass bottles. In addition to this, all the pulp (the part of the vegetable leftover from juicing) is delivered to the Royal Parks in London (Hyde Park, Kensington etc) and used as organic compost. Sustainable initiatives are never the product of one company, if retailers did not make the effort to collect the glass bottles these ideas would never work.

What is your view on sustainability?
For WB&CO, the biggest challenge facing the food industry is food waste. This is not typically seen as a sustainable issue –but it is. Billions of Pounds of food is wasted in the UK and throughout the world each year. This impacts every part of the supply chain and is a contributing factor to the current high cost of food. When we begin to reduce food waste – then we will know that people are starting to value what they are buying. And when they do this, all the other sustainable issues such as primary and secondary packaging etc will reduce. This is what WB&CO will be campaigning for in the future.

What do you dream of for WB&CO?
"Most of all I dream of making vegetable organic products available to as many people as possible. Hopefully we will be able to create enough awareness so people understand why vegetables are so good for them. Our mission is to make vegetables exciting!"

FABULOUS TO SHOP

01. Marqt
02. The People's Supermarket
03. Unpackaged
04. Fishes
05. De Vegetarische Slager
06. Mutterland
07. Lindy & Grundy

01
FABULOUS TO SHOP

Name Marqt
URL marqt.com
Origin The Netherlands

the link between consumer and regional producers of honest, organic products

"Locally grown veg is picked in the morning and by midday it is on our store shelves. With the average supermarket, the gap can easily stretch to 3 days," a passionate Quirijn Bolle explains what he means by delicious, healthy and conscious eating. In 2006, Bolle left a career at Ahold to start his own retail chain. Together with business partner, Meike Beeren, he opened the first two Marqt stores in 2008 and a new breed of supermarket was born. Although Bolle prefers the term marketplace.

How did the idea behind Marqt come about?

My fascination with the food industry began when working for several years at Ahold [a Dutch multinational which owns several supermarket chains] in New York. I realized that the way in which we produce and preserve food is predominantly driven by the principles of cost and efficiency. It has little to do with the spirit that could and in my opinion should be a part of the food we eat. When you look at the industry, you see a relatively short list of large food companies and large retailers. They dominate the market and in so doing form a power block that makes it difficult for small players to gain a foothold. With the immediate consequence that consumers actually have a very limited choice. In the Netherlands, there are only a handful of supermarket chains and they all offer a largely overlapping range. With the result that everyone more or less eats the same thing. It is all mass-produced and comes from the same factory, even fresh produce with a short shelf life that is consequently not really suited to mass production. All kinds of additives are used in an effort to overcome this hurdle: colourings, flavourings, taste-boosters, stabilizers and a whole list of E-numbers that have been approved by the EU but which still raise serious questions in my book. However, all these additives are necessary in order for the produce to satisfy the criteria of the supermarket. As a consequence of the overlapping range of produce, the only thing left for supermarkets to distinguish themselves with is the price. So they build cheaper shops that become eyesores on our streets, where fewer and fewer people work and where knowledge and tradesmanship are slowly disappearing. The drive for innovation is also waning because there is simply no money to innovate.

And you want to change all that?

Yes, because alongside those large producers, there are many, many smaller ones who make beautiful, quality produce that nonetheless never makes it to the supermarket because they cannot meet the capacity requirements. There is a demand for these products but the demand is never satisfied because there is no substantial route connecting the supply with the consumer. For that, a new marketplace was needed: and its name is Marqt.

A new kind of supermarket?

Marqt is more like a genuine marketplace. A place where you can buy great-tasting, healthy and genuinely good food and where

There are producers who take their production process a lot further than the requirements of organic certification and grow wonderful produce that does not have the official label.

local growers, farmers and fishermen are closely involved in the sale of their products. We do not purchase produce but only handle it in exchange for a percentage of the profit. And for that percentage, we play the role of marketplace manager: we take care of the rent, the personnel, the training of the personnel, the sales policy, etc.

Are all the products organic?
Not necessarily. The 'organic' label is not really what whets people's appetite. If the products are grown locally and you know the producers, those labels become a lot less relevant. There are producers who take their production process a lot further than the requirements of organic certification and grow wonderful produce that does not have the official label. Should I then refuse it? Nonsense! Labels can only tell you so much. For items that come from further afield such as olive oil or bread-making flour from France, we do not always know the producers as well and have to rely on labels such as fair trade, organic, Max Havelaar, etc.

Are your products more expensive?
Sometimes, sometimes not. We offer the farmers a direct channel to the consumer so the cut that normally goes to the wholesaler and the packager is eliminated. On top of that, a lot of produce is grown locally which makes for cheaper transport costs.

Imagine listening to a cheese maker tell how he spoils his animals or how the milk changes with the seasons… that is what I mean by 'real'.

Your shops really are a wonderful sight. How did you brief the architect?

Basically, we wanted to see as little shop and as much food as possible. It's all about the food, not Marqt. We definitely do not intend to launch a private label because we do not make our own products. Our briefing therefore stated that we wanted to see as few shelves and racks as possible and a lot of the actual products. We spoke with several architects but very soon got a feeling for whom we wanted to work with. Some came up with intricate, lofty concepts while we were just looking for something simple and authentic. Our first shop in Amsterdam works well but the second one in Haarlem is better. There it has turned into a somewhat rougher marketplace. The fruit crates, for instance, are made from recycled wood that was found lying around at the auction houses. The shelves are also made of used steel that we were able to get our hands on. In my opinion, the Amsterdam shop is just a little bit too "high end", because ultimately it is all about selling everyday produce. For instance, the lettering on the shop window is currently in silver but that is way too chic. That was not a good decision. At first the letters were brown but they were not clearly visible against the reflection of the glass. So we are doing a makeover now.

> Marqt is more like a genuine marketplace. A place where you can buy great-tasting, healthy and genuinely good food and where local growers, farmers and fishermen are closely involved in the sale of their products.

107

You do not want high-end?

No, because we trade in everyday food that is meant to be accessible for everyone. Although at this stage of Marqt's evolution, I realize that our clientele is largely made up of the educated class. We want to bring about a switch in consumer behaviour and you need trendsetters for that who bring the rest of the public in behind them. And those trendsetters are the consumers who are committed and educated, who consciously think about what they eat and understand what Marqt is all about.

What kind of locations do you look for?

Buildings with character, both old and new. Buildings with character, both old and new, which we renovate with total respect for the building and the surrounding neighbourhood. We ask ourselves what characteristics a particular building has and how we can enrich them. Get someone to blindfold you and drive you to any given shopping street in the Netherlands and try and guess what city you are in. You cannot do that anymore. Wherever you go, you end up being surrounded by the same shop fronts. I call that poverty and something that we do not want to be a part of with Marqt.

What is your policy with regards to shop communication?

The bottom line here is that we want all our communications to be relevant for both our customer groups: consumers and producers. Under the motto 'Farmer on the Floor' we regularly invite producers to come in and explain their produce to customers. And we are working on little books per product type (e.g. Cheese, Fish or Meat) in which customers can find more information about the suppliers, how they work, and what distinguishes the products at Marqt from the ones you buy at a regular supermarket. But communication is always subordinate to the produce. So we always restrict ourselves to one specific theme and will never come out with loud mega promotions or fluorescent yellow posters. At present, the price and product info is displayed on discrete boards in black and white. The black and white thing is maybe still a bit high-end but if you put it in a crate of apples, the colour of the produce comes out better and the text is more clearly visible. But in the end, most of the information has to come from the actual product and the shop employees themselves. We have a structured training process to boost the knowledge of our retail staff. There are so many great things to say about the produce in our stores. Imagine listening to a cheese maker tell how he spoils his animals or how the milk changes with the seasons... that is what I mean by 'real'. Not the Italian women in TV ads who stir large pots of soup in Tuscan kitchens, while the actual soup is made in big, grey factories in Poland. At Marqt, it has to be real. Our bread, for instance, is baked four times a day in the shop. The bakery smell, in other words, is real and not from a spray can.

What about your commitment to sustainability? How 'green' is Marqt?

We want to make the whole shopping process as sustainable as possible. We work with local producers, we bring in supplies to our shops using electric lorries, our printing is done on recycled paper and the plastic bags (shoppers) are made of used plastic. Furthermore, we strive to present the products in our shops with as little packaging as possible.

One day we will discover that all those additives and E numbers have a larger impact on our health than we originally thought.

It was not possible to pay with cash at the checkout. What is the reasoning behind that?

Phasing out cash at the shops is about increasing the safety of staff and customers and minimizing the queues and the resulting irritation. We also just have one central queue with lights above each cashier. When the light turns green, the next customer in line can go to the checkout. That means there is never any risk of standing in the wrong line.

In one sentence, how would you describe Marqt's mission?

To make good food every day. In other words, to sell everyday food items that are as good and as original as possible without all manner of additives. This steers you more often than not in the direction of regional produce, because it can be in the shop within a matter of hours. The challenge is to make our customers aware of the fact that good food is important and that food that is sometimes presented as good and reliable may not always be so. One day we will discover that all those additives and E-numbers have a larger impact on our health than we originally thought. The traditional food lobby says that our food has never been safer. That is certainly true with regards to bacteria. But in the meantime, we have lost a whole lot of the beneficial elements of our produce and added things whose long-term effects are still largely unknown. At present, around 1.8% of the food sold in the Netherlands is officially certified as organic. Then there are other products that do not have the label but are produced in a similar way. So let us assume that 2% of the food items sold today are produced in a sustainable way. That 2% should grow to 10% in the future and we want Marqt to be a part of that evolution. In the past, the Ministry of Agriculture has stimulated organic agriculture but nothing has been done to stimulate demand. Up until now, the demand for organic produce has grown little beyond the snobby nature stores.

What about the future? What are your goals?

We currently have three branches, 2 in Amsterdam and 1 in Haarlem. The goal is to grow to 15 shops by 2014, with some in Amsterdam, The Hague, Rotterdam and Utrecht. In addition to that, we have expanded our range in the first half of 2011 by 20%. We want to continue increasing our selection so that we can offer our clients even more daily products. That obviously entails enticing new local suppliers who can agree to Marqt's quality standards.

Where do you get your inspiration?

The 'Zeitgeist'. There are a lot of business concepts that have lasted for a generation but which you feel are approaching the end of their lifecycle. McDonalds might stick around a bit longer because of its name but even they will have to come up with far-reaching innovations in the future. The same goes for the car industry. It is no longer "bigger and faster" but "more economical and better for the environment". The world's population is more than ever ready for innovation and change and this offers a number of inspiring openings in the market. Whole Foods [the American supermarket chain that offers mainly organic produce] is a good example of that new wave. Sometimes I think it can be a bit over the top but the concept is very well thought-out. During my Ahold period in New York, I saw a lot of examples of how things should not be done. And that soon gave rise to ideas about how it should be done. In that respect, the Marqt concept was the obvious next step.

02
FABULOUS TO SHOP

Name: The People's Supermarket
URL: thepeoplessupermarket.org
Origin: United Kingdom

sustainable food cooperative selling local food at reasonable prices

"The People's carrots: These carrots cost a fraction of the price you pay in supermarkets - just because some of them are a fraction of the size. Supermarkets think they're too small but we think size doesn't matter - it's what you do with them that counts. And if you like them we'll get some more in."

On June 5th 2010, after nearly a year of planning, founders Arthur Potts Dawson, Kate Bull and David Barrie agreed they were ready to launch their brand new supermarket concept. "Everyone was complaining about the supermarkets making so much money out of us, but there was no alternative", Potts Dawson says. "Well, now there is."

The People's Supermarket aims to be a commercially sustainable, social enterprise that achieves its growth and profitability targets whilst operating within values based on community development and cohesion. Their intention is to create a parallel food buying network by connecting an urban community with the local farming community. Only a year later, the People's Supermarket has taken over £1,000,000 and serves over 6,000 customers a week, with 1,100 members. And what is more, they are the proud winners of an Observer Ethical Award in the category Local Retailer for 2011. As Arthur Potts Dawson puts it: "It is all about good food for and by the people."

What is the idea behind The People's Supermarket?

The Supermarket is a sustainable food cooperative that responds to the needs of the local community and provides healthy, local food at reasonable prices. Each one of the founders has unique business skills. My background is in retailing and the insights I gained helped us to develop the right business model. We are not just three nice people with an idea, we just used a traditional supermarket business plan and enhanced it to drive our business forward.

How does it work?

It is a completely new way of doing your shopping. It is about good food at affordable prices. But to get the cheap food - 10% discount off your shopping bills - you have to become a member. Anyone can join The People's Supermarket, but each member is committed to working in the shop for 4 hours a month. Because the work force is nearly all volunteers, we are saving on staff costs and that means your shopping is cheaper. Any profits we make go back into making the food even more affordable.

Who decides how the supermarket runs?

The members do. Because The People's Supermarket belongs to them, it is not just about shopping and working there. It is about having a say in how it works, what kind of food we sell and, ultimately, what kind of shop it should be.

What is the People's Supermarket's mission?

We wanted to create a supermarket that meets the needs of its members and the local community by offering high quality, healthy food at reasonable prices. We want to buy from trusted suppliers with whom we develop mutually sustaining relationships. We want to buy British produce where possible, and produce local to London. We want to minimise wastage, by creating prepared dishes in The People's Kitchen from food coming up to its sell-by date, and by composting all other waste material. We want to provide inspirational training and life skill opportunities to the local community.

The People's Supermarket

OWNED BY THE PEOPLE, FOR THE PEOPLE
WWW.THEPEOPLESSUPERMARKET.ORG

How do you select your suppliers?

They must meet our criteria and our first port of call is always local sustainable suppliers. Our bread comes from a bakery down the road from the supermarket, our pasta is locally made in North London by a small Italian family business and all our fruit and vegetables are seasonal ensuring the freshest and best quality produce for our customers and members.

You have an event called Supper Club. What does it stand for?

The People's Supper Club was the brainchild of the chefs in the People's Kitchen. They aim to create evenings of inspired food using the best of British ingredients and produce from the supermarket, which would otherwise go to waste. Including some interesting bin end sourced wines. We launched our first People's Supper Club in April. It took place in the store. The dining in the aisles Supper Club events take place every two months and are open to both members and non-members of the supermarket. We serve a four-course meal, cocktails, wine, coffee and petit fours, limited to 50 people.

What are your plans for the future?

By 2012, we intend to grow the movement and encourage more people to shop at local co-ops. We hope to see our sales increase to £1.4 million by selling more products from more suppliers to more members. We are aiming at 2000 members by then. Also, we plan to provide training and social events that engage the local community. Our longer term plans include more branded products, cookery books, delivery bikes and a training academy. And of course, to develop our model for others to roll out around the UK.

03
FABULOUS TO SHOP

Name **Unpackaged**
URL **beunpackaged.com**
Origin **United Kingdom**

shop groceries using your own containers

What is the first thing you do when you get home from the supermarket? Unpack your groceries and throw away the packaging, right? A bit strange, to say the least. That is exactly what Catherine Conway used to think. Because it was impossible for her to go shopping using her own containers, she started a grocery shop, filled it up with unpackaged products and invited customers to bring their own bags, jars, bottles, tupperware, or whatever it is they use at home. Catherine set up Unpackaged in 2007. And people got the message…

Catherine encourages sustainable behaviour even before consuming has started. "Precycling", they call it, and it is about reducing waste before it has even been produced. Recycling is not always the solution. True, some packaging is recycled, but even then most ends up in landfill sites anyway. "Recycling is certainly part of the solution, but it will only work if we use less packaging and adopt more 'reusable' ways of doing things – Unpackaged is based on this ethos".

Unpackaged opened in 2007. How did it all start?

Unpackaged began because I, as a consumer, wanted to be able to refill my weekly groceries. I used to refill Ecover eco cleaning products in a local Buddhist shop, but did not understand why I could not refill everything that way… I spent a year working on the idea before receiving a small amount of social enterprise funding to try the idea on a market stall. After a year and two market stalls, we opened the shop.

What is the idea behind your concept?

We sell high quality, organic food and environmentally sustainable household products in refills, enabling customers to bring their own containers to fill up their

> Recycling is certainly part of the solution, but it will only work if we use less packaging and adopt more 'reusable' ways of doing things – Unpackaged is based on this ethos.

weekly groceries and reduce packaging waste. Our vision is a world with less packaging and we are achieving it one customer at a time!

What happens when people forget to bring their containers?

That happens of course, especially with new customers who are not yet familiar with the concept. In that case, they can buy reusable containers in the store.

What is the problem with packaging?

Whilst some packaging is necessary in our modern industrialised food chain, unnecessary packaging is a waste. It increases the price of the goods you buy because you are charged twice, first when you buy overpackaged products and then through council tax for disposing of your rubbish. Secondly, it wastes resources at every level; production, storage, transport and disposal. Finally, landfill and incineration are the two main ways of dealing with un-recyclable packaging waste. These are major pollutants for people and the environment as they release greenhouse gases.

What can you buy at Unpackaged?

We are a small organic grocery selling everything from daily essentials (bread, milk, eggs, fruit & veg) to store cupboard items (tea, coffee, wholefoods, nuts, herbs & spices) to deli products (wine and cheese) to household and body care products (cleaners, washing up liquids, shampoo), all loose and refillable. We work directly with producers to source everything as locally and seasonally as possible.

We help people save money and save the environment.

Reduce by only buying what you need
Reuse by bringing your containers for a refill
Recycle what you can't reuse
And... if you can't reuse or recycle it
then don't buy it!

Who shops at Unpackaged?
A range of people, from local residents who come because we are the local shop, to committed environmentalists who come from further away because we provide a packaging free solution. They are united by their commitment to good food and doing what they can to help the environment. We consider everyone to be on a spectrum to becoming a committed refiller. Some people walk in and it is the shop they dreamed of, others are new to the idea, but most can see that it is common sense once we have explained it!

Are there things that you want to change or improve, short term?
We are always improving things – for example we are currently debating getting rid of any bottled wine and only selling refills with bottles… And whether we should charge for paper bags.

Unpackaged literally reduces waste, but at the same time, it is a statement. Is the shop an educational tool for the community?
We were conceived as a social enterprise. At the heart of Unpackaged is the social/environmental message that makes us both the message and the messenger. Our mission statement clearly positions us a campaigning business. As such, we provide much more than just a business. We are a focus for community involvement – such as hosting groups from local schools who are learning about reuse and recycling.

You did not make a lot of changes to the shop, was that a deliberate choice?
Our property is a Grade 2 listed building meaning that the interior and exterior are

protected as a heritage building and cannot be changed. Not that we would want to! Our aim was to 'reuse' an old building as part of our overall aim. The whole interior was designed with our partners Multistorey to reflect our aims. The tubs were designed to fit in with the old interior, adding to rather than bulldozing over and everything was designed with sustainability in mind. For example, our signage is designed to be able to be written over whenever we need to rather than continually printing out new signs.

You ask people to get involved? Why is that?

Unpackaged is a group project led by me – over the years friends and strangers have generously donated their time, skills and energy to make Unpackaged happen – architects, designers, copyrighters, branding experts, lawyers, all united by the fact that they want to see Unpackaged, as a concept, succeed. We get a range of volunteers, from MBA's working on enterprise projects to people who just want to help out in the shop. Bartering time is the oldest form of human trade – anyone can do it so we welcome any help we can get.

Any plans for the future?

Lots! We are moving to a bigger space that will include a cafe and will be better designed, using all the knowledge we have gained over 4 years of refilling. In turn this will create a model that we can help people replicate in their own communities. Internally we are also working on product design – designing refillable products to encourage other shops to go unpackaged.

> Unpackaged is about rewarding people for re-using their containers and doing their bit to tackle our wasteful culture.

04
FABULOUS TO SHOP

Name **Fishes**
URL **fishes.nl**
Origin **The Netherlands**

fish and fish products from sustainable fisheries

Even as a boy, Bart van Olphen somehow knew he was destined for a career in food. He began his own catering company during his studies at the Hospitality College before becoming an assistant chef at a starred restaurant, a marketer of Ben & Jerry's ice cream and director of an Amsterdam club. In between all this he came close to being an inspector for Michelin as well. It was in 2002, however, that this culinary entrepreneur founded Van Olphen Fishes, a new breed of seafood shop that was to blow a breath of fresh air through the otherwise rather stuffy and traditional seafood trade. The company has since become a pioneer in the domain of quality seafood with five retail outlets and wholesale contracts with a number of supermarkets throughout Europe. What began as just another project in 2002 has, in other words, become a true calling. "In 5 years time we hope to be able to say that the fisheries are growing again and that Fishes has played a pioneering role in that growth."

Our story is the story of small boats moored on the beach at Hastings, pushed into the water before dawn and dew by three fishermen to return a few hours later carrying a few crates of sole.

Papa van Olphen was an architect and made an effort to show his two sons and daughter Europe's most beautiful buildings. "We always took time out on our journeys for a delicious meal in one of those classic restaurants with prim waiters and white table cloths," tells Bart. "It was always my dream from a young age to start such a restaurant of my own." Until, that is, he ended up in Lucas Carton's kitchen in Paris years later. For eight months, Van Olphen worked at this top restaurant with three Michelin stars. "After that, I knew one thing for certain: this was not what I wanted. For my part, there was room for more sparkle and less conservatism."

What was the next step, then?
"After that I became the director of Vakzuid in Amsterdam, a trendy club slash restaurant established in the mid 1990s and a real beacon of innovation on the scene at the time. Vakzuid was certainly an eye-opener for me. It showed me that the restaurant business could always be done differently. Not only in terms of the menu but also at the level of décor and service."

What was the idea behind Fishes?
"At Vakzuid we saw that there was a high demand for seafood. We were serving around 300 covers a day and at least 50% of them were for seafood. The most popular numbers were tuna, monkfish and cockles. When I realised that these varieties were not exactly available from the local fish shop, I got thinking. Alongside the old-fashioned offering, there was also something wrong with the décor of those typical Dutch seafood shops. That omnipresent smell of fried fish and the typical drain in the middle of the floor. If you ask me, there was room for a different approach."

In five years time, we hope to see fishery stocks increasing again and to be able to say that Fishes played a pioneering role in achieving that result.

So how did you see things, concretely?

"I do not just want to sell fish, I want to sell the whole experience of the sea, the fish and the fishermen. Fishes actually wants to reconnect the fisherman and the consumer and to make the process entirely transparent, all the way from the boat to the shop. Our consumers can even communicate directly with the fishing communities online. That kind of transparency is very uncommon in the fishing industry. To be honest, I do not see myself as a marketer, I am a storyteller.

Were there other shops at the time that inspired you?

"In 2001 I was in Dean&Deluca in New York and thought it was fantastic. Everything worked: the people, the shelves, the products… I was there again last year, though, and that wow feeling had all but gone. But I get it again whenever I walk into Wholefoods."

I had a very clear idea of what the Fishes shops should look like. I wanted to get that pure, romantic image of the fish market back into the shop. Everything had to be on offer, too: not just seafood but also wine, olive oil, crockery, cooking books, serving dishes, etc. And behind the counter came chefs who could tell customers how to cook their fish. The philosophy, from the very beginning, was to keep all permanent fixtures in a sober grey with both the products and the people in colour. That was the best way to accentuate that pure and natural feeling that is part and parcel of fish and the fish market. Studio Linse developed the idea further into the shops you see today."

Do you change the design of the shops on a regular basis?
"We are constantly thinking about improvements. The shop in Amsterdam-South, for instance, has been given a complete makeover. But we are not there yet. I want to create even more unity and uniformity. And the experience has to come across more, I think. The same goes for the packaging. We gradually evolved towards more black on the wine bottles, olive oil and mayonnaise. I want every product in our shop to have the same style of label."

You also sell to supermarkets. What is your packaging philosophy there?
"We have just restyled our packaging. It is in basic black and white, with only the Fishes 'F' in colour. We have 13 different colours that all refer to a specific fishery. Here, too, the experience is primary. That was our starting point: the packaging tells the story of the fisheries and the fishermen."

> It is pretty simple, actually: we want to sell really good fish. From that point of view, the sustainability story becomes self-evident.

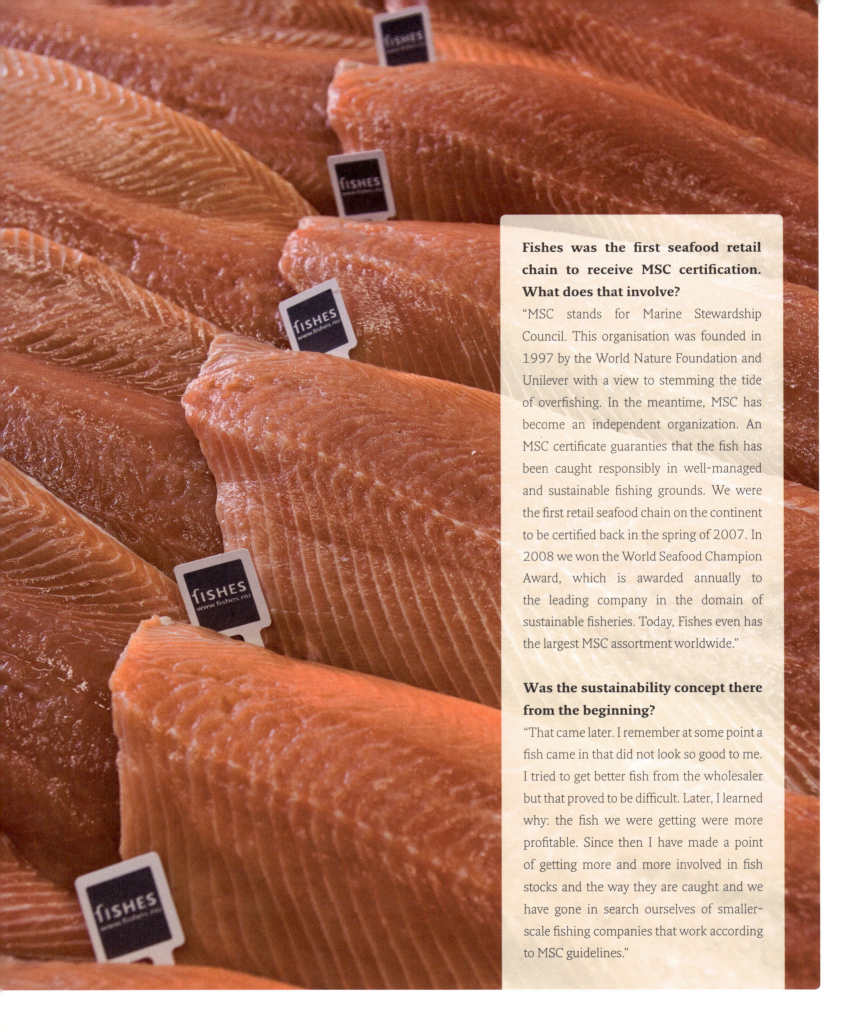

Fishes was the first seafood retail chain to receive MSC certification. What does that involve?

"MSC stands for Marine Stewardship Council. This organisation was founded in 1997 by the World Nature Foundation and Unilever with a view to stemming the tide of overfishing. In the meantime, MSC has become an independent organization. An MSC certificate guaranties that the fish has been caught responsibly in well-managed and sustainable fishing grounds. We were the first retail seafood chain on the continent to be certified back in the spring of 2007. In 2008 we won the World Seafood Champion Award, which is awarded annually to the leading company in the domain of sustainable fisheries. Today, Fishes even has the largest MSC assortment worldwide."

Was the sustainability concept there from the beginning?

"That came later. I remember at some point a fish came in that did not look so good to me. I tried to get better fish from the wholesaler but that proved to be difficult. Later, I learned why: the fish we were getting were more profitable. Since then I have made a point of getting more and more involved in fish stocks and the way they are caught and we have gone in search ourselves of smaller-scale fishing companies that work according to MSC guidelines."

Real commitment or clever marketing?

"It is pretty simple, actually: we want to sell really good fish. From that point of view, the sustainability story becomes self-evident. But we do not make it a marketing message. We are not saying: buy sustainable fish! We are saying: buy good quality fish! Our story is the story of small boats moored on the beach at Hastings, pushed into the water before dawn and dew by three fishermen to return a few hours later carrying a few crates of sole. That is in stark contrast to the mega trawlers that haul tonnes of fish out of the sea, of which a considerable amount is incidental catch which is thrown back. Our story leads almost by definition to good quality fish and is only accentuated by the certification. Of course it is an added bonus marketing-wise that we appear in a newspaper or magazine every week with an interesting story about sustainability and fair trade.

The philosophy, from the very beginning, was to keep all permanent fixtures in a sober grey with both the products and the people in colour. That was the best way to accentuate that pure and natural feeling that is part and parcel of fish and the fish market.

I do not just want to sell fish, I want to sell the whole experience of the sea, the fish and the fishermen.

Fishes is not just a retail chain but also a wholesaler. How did that come about?

"We launched the wholesale side of the business in March 2007. I was in London one day eating a bowl of pasta for lunch and read an article about a fishing community in Hastings. I was so inspired by the story that I decided to go there straightaway. The journey ended in a tiny little office where the fishermen told me with great enthusiasm how good their produce was but how little they got for it at the local auction. A week later I had sold a lot of theirs to the supermarket chain Albert Heijn and our wholesale division was born. Not that we did not have enough on our plate with our own shops, but I saw an opportunity that I could not let slip. The advantage of being a wholesaler is that you turn over greater volumes which makes it easier to develop a franchise at retail level. You cannot have everything custom made for just five shops."

How did you get your foot in the door with the big supermarkets as a relatively small player?

"We have a story that no one else can tell. We work with sustainable fishing companies. That costs a lot of extra time and effort if you compare it to the relatively small volumes such companies supply. No other wholesaler does that. But at the same time, the supermarkets are feeling increasing pressure from NGOs and the government to sell more sustainable fish. And then we come along in our jeans and no tie and everything falls into place. And we do not just sell to supermarkets. Our fish is also served on board KLM aircraft!"

Do you advertise?

"Up until now we have not done very much advertising. We did something in ELLE because our cans of salmon and tuna are three times the price of ordinary cans. As a consequence you have to explain why that is the case. Also, we published Fish Tales, a mix of recipes and information about the sustainable fisheries we work with. English chef Tom Kime and I follow the fishermen and cook delectable dishes from their catch. The book was released in the US, The Netherlands, England, South Africa and Australia. In 2010, it won the "Gourmand

We have a story that no one else can tell. We work with sustainable fishing companies. That costs a lot of extra time and effort if you compare it to the relatively small volumes such companies supply. No other wholesaler does that.

World Cookbook Award" for best sustainable cookbook in the world. The concept has been discussed with a television production company that is interested in turning it into an eight part TV series. I strongly believe in this kind of publicity because we are able to convey our story very clearly without it being preachy or irritating. We are currently working on our next book about small sustainable African fishing communities in Mauritania, Madagascar, Kenya etc. It is not only about sustainable fish, it covers the social aspects as well. We cook together with the fishermen en listen to their stories. And recently, we published 'Het Nederlands Viskookboek' (The Dutch Fish Cookbook) which tells the story of Dutch sustainable fishes and how to prepare them.

What do you plan to do with Fishes in the future?

"MSC state in their most recent annual report that the amount of MSC certified produce on the Dutch market rose by 2200% last year. At least half of that increase is a direct result of our efforts. I want to push this evolution in the rest of Europe. In five years time, we hope to see fishery stocks increasing again and to be able to say that Fishes played a pioneering role in achieving that result. Hopefully that will go hand in hand with an increase in Fishes' brand recognition. We want to launch the brand throughout Europe, in South Africa, the US and the Middle East.

05
FABULOUS TO SHOP

Name De Vegetarische Slager
URL devegetarischeslager.nl
Origin The Netherlands

plant-based butchery products

No meat substitute has so far been able to tempt hard-line meat eaters to put aside their favourite food, even for a single day. That was before Jaap Korteweg, founder of De Vegetarische Slager (The Vegetarian Butcher), arrived on the scene. He has made it his mission to come up with plant-based butcher-style products that will make people forget about 'real' meat. What he sells tastes like meat, but it contains no meat.

Jaap Korteweg is an organic arable farmer. This has not always been the case, because his parents ran a mixed farm. After the outbreak of swine fever in 1997, however, he decided to become a vegetarian. It was not easy considering that he is a great meat lover, and meat is difficult to replace. His search for a plant-based alternative with the same texture and flavour, and the same "bite" as meat has driven him forward, creating the basis for De Vegetarische Slager. "That empty place on the plate needs to be filled with a product that comes as close to it as possible," says Korteweg. "The taste-experience is key." He does not want meat-eaters to have the feeling that they need to sacrifice something if they go without meat for a few days. Jaap Korteweg found the solution: lupins.

Like soya, the lupin plant has beans from which a fibre can be produced with a firm bite and a nutty flavour that can serve as a basis for all kinds of dishes. With the help of scientists and top cooks, Korteweg further improved his concept. Lupin is a good meat substitute because, like meat, it is rich in protein. It is also a sustainable product. The robust lupin is highly suitable for organic growing without the use of artificial fertilisers or chemical agents. It is easy to grow locally, while soya has to be imported from South America. And it requires much less energy and water than meat production. 1 kg of beans is used to make 3 kg of product. If you translate that into meat, 1 kg of beans corresponds to 200 g of meat. "The challenge for me was to make delicious satays, kebabs, burgers and sausages directly from healthy and nutritious lupin beans rather than via animals." In 2006 Jaap Korteweg began growing lupins on four organic farms. Four years later, on 2 October 2010, the first Vegetarische Slager opened its doors in The Hague.

Just under a year after the opening, De Vegetarische Slager won the first Hart-Hoofd (Heart-Head) prize for the most innovative and inspiring sustainable entrepreneur from Dutch Triodos Bank. The cash prize will be used to continue developing the products and enlarging the range. 100% plant-based Rookworst (smoked sausage) is at the top of the list. Meat substitutes have long been seen as second-class products, but that seems to be changing now. If Ferran Adrià from restaurant El Bulli is an enthusiast, then things are moving in the right direction. Jaap Korteweg wants to bring De Vegetarische Slager to the whole of Europe and make the products accessible to a wide public. "The aim is to replace as much chicken, pork, beef and lamb with purely plant-based products as possible. If you can give people tastier food that they enjoy, whilst doing something positive for animals, nature, the climate, the environment, the world food problem and their own health, that could mean a breakthrough that would make the world look very different."

131

06
FABULOUS TO SHOP

Name **Mutterland**
URL **mutterland.de**
Origin **Germany**

> The name Mutterland is a nostalgic reference to the constant love of our mothers and to Germany itself.

artisan delicatessen from mother Germany

The Bieberhuis, a wonderfully restored building dating from 1909 close to Hamburg railway station, is home to Mutterland, a delicatessen and café specialising in traditional artisanal products and dishes. The name Mutterland is a nostalgic reference to the constant love of our mothers and to Germany itself. Virtually everything on sale here comes from German soil and it is all produced responsibly. Many products come from Hamburg and the surrounding area.

When designer and food enthusiast Jan Schawe started his business in 2007 in the midst of the crisis, people close to him were doubtful. Nevertheless, he believed in his concept and pressed on. There is no better remedy for the crisis than to support the German economy, he must have thought. In November 2009 a second store was opened in the centre of Hamburg, followed by a third in Hamburg Eppendorf in the autumn of 2010.

Whether they are branded goods or own brand, most of the food products at Mutterland are "made in Germany": handmade Slow Food jam, natural honey from northern and eastern Germany, fine artisanal chocolates and pralines, delicious old-fashioned sweets, organic wines from young winemakers, dairy products, meat and vegetables from organic farmers and much more. You can also come to Mutterland for a roll, a snack, soups, salads and cooked meals, which you can either eat in the café or take away. Here you will find traditional German food, prepared freshly every day in the kitchen in Hamburg, using the best ingredients and following time-honoured recipes. Just like your mother used to make it. Schawe wanted his delicatessen business to look different and to go against the flow of the large chains with no identity. When

Whether they are branded goods or own brand, most of the food products at Mutterland are "made in Germany".

Mutterland is nostalgia, sustainable nostalgia.

you walk into Mutterland, you somehow feel as if you are coming home. There is something familiar and comforting about it. The beautifully packaged artisanal products, the specially designed shelves made of stacked vegetable boxes and the bric-a-brac furniture create a sense of longing for bygone days. Mutterland is nostalgia, sustainable nostalgia.

Jan Schawe only works with carefully selected small and medium-sized producers, the vast majority of whom buy selected organic products from sustainable farms. The problem is that in Germany you can only call a product organic if it has a biolabel, and to get this label the producer has to satisfy a wide range of requirements. Often this is not feasible for small farms, even though they produce their food organically and sustainably. All homemade dishes and drinks at Mutterland do have the biolabel. Products from large international food chains that have to be transported from the other side of the world to Germany and whose origin is difficult to trace, have no place here. Unless there is no alternative, of course. When it comes to fruit and vegetables, the seasons are always taken into account. Jan Schawe: "Wherever possible we try to avoid long transport routes, even within Germany. We do not have to bring bread or milk from the other end of the country if we can get it from local organic farmers at a reasonable price. Less transport is good for the environment, and we are also supporting the local economy. After all, the further it travels, the less remains for the producer."

When you walk into Mutterland, you somehow feel as if you are coming home.

Products from large international food chains that have to be transported from the other side of the world to Germany and whose origin is difficult to trace, have no place here.

07
FABULOUS TO SHOP

Name **Lindy & Grundy**
URL **lindyandgrundy.com**
Origin **USA**

Summer 2010: Amelia "Lindy" Posada and Erika "Grundy" Nakamura leave their home in New York and cross America from East to West with their great dream: to open the first sustainable nose-to-tail butcher shop in Los Angeles. They start their road trip with nothing but a rental agreement. People follow the whole route on Twitter. Their wedding in Connecticut, the first state border they cross, where they eat and with whom, their wedding reception in Santa Barbara, their vision, their goal, their story - they tweet about everything. Even before they arrive in LA they have a whole community behind them, from food bloggers to potential customers, impatiently looking forward to the opening of Lindy & Grundy, Local, Pastured and Organic Meats. In April 2011 it finally happens.

nose-to-tail butcher shop selling local, pasture-raised, organic meat

They are not your average butchers - both of them have been vegetarians for years - but two rock 'n roll butcherettes who have found each other in love and share their passion for food, their rejection of the meat industry and their powerful commitment to sustainability. Erika Nakamura used to work as a cook but felt that her vocation was elsewhere and went to train with top butcher Fleischer's Grass-fed & Organic Meats in Brooklyn, New York. It was here that she first had the idea for Lindy & Grundy. She persuaded her partner Amelia Posada, who had been working as a floral designer, to become a butcher too so that they could start up a small sustainable butcher shop in Los Angeles together.

In every other butcher shop in Los Angeles the meat arrives already cut and packaged. As a result, any link to its origin is completely lost. At Lindy & Grundy only 'whole' animals come in. They are broken down on the premises and processed from nose to tail. Nothing is added whatsoever: no preservatives, no water, it is pure meat. Everything is done in-house and nothing is wasted. Even the offcuts are used as dog treats.

The entire process is sustainable. Amelia and Erika only work with small family farms which are at a distance of no more than 150 miles (240 km) from Los Angeles. This helps them to reduce their ecological footprint and support the local economy. Their collaboration with ranchers is based

on mutual trust. They know every animal's history and share it with their customers. On the farms these animals are fed exclusively on grass. They have room to graze peacefully and walk around freely and they are raised naturally, with no hormones or antibiotics at all. That has an effect on the quality of the meat. They even visited the abattoirs before they started to make sure that the animals are dispatched in an animal-friendly way.
Lindy & Grundy hark back to the old days, the friendly old-fashioned butcher around the corner who knew all their customers by name. The meat is more expensive but its quality makes up for that.

We would love to meat you

FABULOUS TO FARM

01. Dakboerin

02. PlantLab

03. Allotinabox

04. Willem & Drees

05. GRO Holland

01
FABULOUS TO FARM

Name **Dakboerin**
URL **dakboerin.nl**
Origin **The Netherlands**

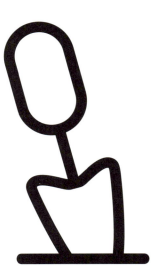

vegetable gardens on rooftops in urban areas

Since 1 January 2011 Annelies Kuiper has been known as Dakboerin (Rooftop Farmer) - the first in the Netherlands - and has spent her time transforming unused city roofs into attractive vegetable gardens. A vegetable garden on your roof has all the advantages of an ordinary green roof, with one additional benefit: you can eat it. "From your roof to your plate."

Starting with her own roof, which served as a test case, she set out on her mission to conquer colourless flat roofs, with the occasional sideways excursion along the way. At the Dutch music and cultural festival Lowlands 2011 she helped to build a vertical garden, an impressive scaffolding structure consisting of 375 crates filled with herbs and vegetables.

Annelies had long been interested in sustainable lifestyles and organic food, but some time ago she also developed a fascination with urban agriculture. People today are living more consciously, eating more healthily and want to know where their food comes from, so there is a growing demand for locally grown organic products. Now they are looking for ways to bring agriculture into cities. Dakboerin meets this need perfectly: "Land is scarce in urban areas, but roofs... there are plenty of those."

How exactly does Dakboerin work?

First of all I provide a design based on the roof owner's requirements, taking into account the roof surface and its structure. I then create the roof garden and maintain it if required. Food harvested from the roof can be prepared immediately in the company canteen, restaurant, school canteen or under your own roof at home.

I use organic seeds and plants, soft fruit bushes and fruit trees. They are all planted in a lightweight natural substrate. I get help from experts to assess the roof structure, supply the subsoil, apply for licenses and subsidies and design items like sheds, beehives and mobile chicken runs.

How did you arrive at the idea?

I have been interested in sustainable lifestyles, authentic eating and growing vegetables for a long time. It is the combination of city and country that excites me most. A new concept such as roof gardening for an old activity like growing food is quite a challenge. Last summer I was reading about empty buildings and the fact that eating organic food is becoming more important for more and more people. Well, I put the two together. The sustainability aspect came later: green roofs are better for the city because they store water, absorb CO2 and create a greener, cooler environment (insulation). What is more, a roof like this lasts 30 years longer.

Which roofs are suitable?

Of course you can go from 1m2 in a box up to 10,000 m2. The condition is that it must be a flat roof and the structure must be able to support the weight. What you actually do is adapt your roof garden to suit the roof structure. As you can imagine, cabbages that put down deep roots will not do well in 20cm

of soil. They will need at least 50cm, but that also makes the garden a lot heavier. I started out with my own roof above my kitchen. That is 12 m2 and it feeds two people from spring to autumn. This winter I will be putting up cold frames so that I can have more of my own vegetables in the winter too.

How much does a rooftop garden cost?
You should allow between 90 and 125 euro per m2 for installation. That is more expensive than a regular roof, but it is much more sustainable because your roof will last longer and it will also be much more attractive, for example if you should sell your house at some point. Over a number of years, an edible roof works out cheaper than a bitumen roof. Not to mention the vegetables that you grow yourself and therefore do not need to buy in the shops. That saves money too...

What can you grow or keep on a roof?
In principle you can grow anything on a roof, as long as you have a good structure with a deep layer of substrate on top, which is soil composed of lightweight material that absorbs water more effectively.

The ideal vegetable roof incorporates a number of different cycles: you collect rainwater and use it to water your garden, you compost your vegetable waste after harvesting, cooked waste goes to the chickens, the chickens peck amongst the larger plants and fertilise parts of the garden, and bees pollinate the plants.

What are the advantages of having a vegetable garden on the roof?
I think the greatest benefit is that when it is time to prepare a meal you can have a look on the roof and see what is ready to harvest. Looking around you see the other roofs with their bitumen or green coverings or solar panels, and feel a sense of peace. You harvest what you need and half an hour later your roof vegetables are on the table downstairs in a pleasant, cool environment because your vegetable roof has provided such good insulation. Food does not come more local than that. You do not have to worry about opening times or cycle off to your allotment.

What are the main differences from creating an ordinary vegetable garden?
You get a wonderful view from your vegetable garden. You have fewer problems with slugs, weeds and fungi. You have to climb upstairs to get to your garden. The elements such as the rain, sun and wind are more extreme when you are high up. As a rooftop farmer, I take these factors into account at the design stage.

Does it require a major commitment from the owner of a roof garden?
Gardening is mostly about relaxation, whether it is on the roof or in the garden. Some people play football with friends, others take courses in painting and still others enjoy creating a vegetable garden. Football helps you to get fit and a painter has pleasant views to look at but a gardener gets fit and enjoys pleasant views too, and he has home-grown vegetables to put on the table every day as well.

So what do you grow on your roof?

On my first roof I have got a lot of diversity: pumpkins, chard, kale, potatoes, lettuces, tomatoes, strawberries, parsnips, carrots, sprouts, artichokes, leeks, cauliflower, nasturtiums, pot marigolds, French marigolds, Chinese cabbage, sweetcorn and runner beans. I have the same conditions downstairs as the roof upstairs, because there is a concrete base underneath. There are grapes, horseradish, mint, lemon balm, sage, rhubarb, red cabbage, cauliflower, Savoy cabbage, celeriac and fennel. In winter of course I have winter cabbage, and in the cold frame on the roof there is also spinach, turnip greens, lettuce, winter purslane, chard and rocket.

Do you think Urban Farming will be a necessity in future, looking at the environment and the need to supply food to cities?

Eight to ten percent of all fruit and vegetables could be sourced from cities. I think there really needs to be some interaction between what happens in the city and in the surrounding area. There are a number of inescapable factors that are becoming more and more important. Consumers want transparency; they want to know where their food comes from. Food kilometres are important: consumers prefer to buy local and regional rather than international. People are eating a healthier diet. Increasingly they are choosing organic products that do the least possible damage to the environment and respect animal habitats. That does of course include rooftop gardening, as well as making use of empty buildings and unused land. The advantage is that in this way knowledge about food and food production can find its way back into the city. Knowledge means that consumers will become more independent

Green roofs are better for the city because they store water, absorb CO_2 and create a greener, cooler environment.

You harvest what you need and half an hour later your roof vegetables are on the table downstairs.

of large food producers and adopt a more critical approach. Have a look at the film Food Inc.; that is an example of how things should not be done.

Were you already interested in Urban Farming before?

Yes, I had been following urban farming for a while, and some interesting reports have been coming out of the WUR (University of Wageningen). The Marconi project in Rotterdam, using a plot of unused land for temporary agriculture, and the experiments at Aquaponics - growing vegetables and farming fish simultaneously in a greenhouse - both attracted my interest.

Is Dakboerin a completely sustainable and organic concept?

It is not yet possible to be completely sustainable, because rooftop farming is about investments that a customer needs to make in his roof. Sometimes things are not available or there is such a large difference in price that the customer chooses less sustainable materials. I do use organic seeds and plants and a natural substrate. The organic aspect is very important for me. This way of growing food does the least possible damage to the earth, gets the best out of the vegetables and produces the highest nutritional value. Dakboerin prefers to use recycled materials or materials that can be recycled.

> Eight to ten percent of all fruit and vegetables could be sourced from cities.

There is more air pollution in cities; are you not concerned that this will affect the concept?

The plants use CO2, which is yet another cycle. Some gardeners want to have more CO2 in their greenhouses to stimulate plant growth. The majority of the problem with particulate materials comes from other countries. Influences from the continent are responsible for 73% of this, and we cause the rest ourselves through soot emissions, industry and agriculture. Natural resources do of course play their part too. The air above the North Sea is quite salty and regularly blows inland.

All public authorities acknowledge that particulate materials are a major problem. That is another reason why green roofs and vertical gardens have become popular with municipal and provincial authorities. Plants are able to take up particulate materials via their stomas and roots. When it rains, they are washed off the leaves. In this way they purify the air. They absorb hardly any particulate materials at all.

Six months after starting, you had already won a Biodiversity Innovation Award in the 2011 New Venture business competition, which will no doubt be a major encouragement to keep going. What is Dakboerin's dream?

Yes, of course the prize was wonderful, especially hearing that people think it is such a great idea. In fact, that is a big part of what having a vegetable roof is about: the idea that you are growing your own vegetables on your own roof. Dakboerin dreams of having a number of rooftop farms to bring the production as close to the market as possible. That means using the vegetables from the roof in the restaurant downstairs or by a caterer inside the building, in a large company canteen, etc. As a rooftop farmer you are not only interested in growing vegetables and the plants that support them, but you want to know what will happen to those vegetables too: eating, preserving, spreading knowledge about growing vegetables, the nutrients in food and what they do to people. What I would really like is to have a rooftop farming company that makes the whole food chain visible: from producing seeds right up to the toilets where those vegetables ultimately end up (laughs)!

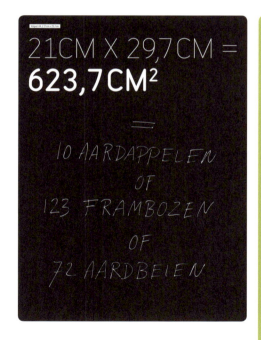

02
FABULOUS TO FARM

Name **PlantLab**
URL **plantlab.nl**
Origin **The Netherlands**

indoor vertical farming with Led-light

When you open the door of a Plant Production Unit, you are bathed in a purplish-red glow: this is the heart of PlantLab. Until recently plants were only grown outdoors or in traditional greenhouses. The result: too much light, too little light, too hot, too cold, too dry, too wet, but never just right. PlantLab takes a different approach. The team at PlantLab comprises John van Gemert, Marcel Kers and Gertjan Meeuws, three horticultural engineers, and Leon Van Duijn, a technical engineer. He bridges the gap between plants and technology. The four of them have been working on this project for several years, motivated by ecological and social considerations and a strong desire to innovate. Together they have achieved a world first: in their Plant Paradise they have succeeded in growing not only salad vegetables and decorative plants but also fruit-bearing plants, using no daylight, with nothing but red & blue LED light. Something considered impossible in expert circles. There are tomatoes, peppers, courgettes, sweetcorn, beans, cucumbers and even strawberries. It opens up prospects ranging from vertical farming in rapidly growing urban areas to supplying food to developing countries. For PlantLab, the world is not enough …

What is PlantLab?

PlantLab has developed a new nursery in which plants are grown in multiple layers (vertical farming) using only LED light. In other words, no daylight is used. These nurseries can be made as small as a microwave oven or airing cupboard, or as large as a block of flats with tens of thousands square metres of growing space. We call them Plant Paradise, because they are a place where we are trying to make these plants as happy as possible. Plants are very intelligent organisms, capable of making seeds and creating a new generation even in unfavourable conditions. As a result, they can achieve much more in Paradise than they can in nature. Since plants are so happy in Plant Paradise, they are not susceptible to diseases and pests. We have never had to use pesticides! What is more, we use almost no water, saving more than 90% in comparison with traditional growing techniques. And it can be done anywhere: in the Arctic Circle, at the equator and in a city centre. Every aspect can be planned and the food is tasty and healthier than what we are currently used to!

This can be done anywhere: in the Arctic Circle, at the equator and in the city centre. Every aspect can be planned.

Why is less water needed?

Plants cool themselves by taking up water through their roots, which evaporates again via the leaves. We collect all the evaporated water and it drains back into the water tank. As a result we do not lose any water through evaporation.

How did the idea come about?

During the 1990s, we monitored more than 500 plant measurement fields with different horticultural crops and used that knowledge to develop mathematical production and prediction models. Through this process we found that plants were capable of much more than we had previously been able to achieve. We saw the shortcomings of growing plants both outdoors and in existing greenhouses and focused on developing a new kind of nursery. A new building, designed like a tailor-made suit around the plant: Plant Paradise.

What are the advantages of this growing method in terms of sustainability?

This way of growing plants creates tremendous opportunities ranging from urban market gardeners improving and refining their own products through contact with their customers, to nurseries for rapidly developing cities in China. In many cases production is already three times higher than a modern greenhouse. What is more, we use hardly any water, obtain energy from alternative sources and work without pesticides. Since this can be done anywhere in the world, growing food locally becomes obvious. And the vegetables are not only sustainably grown and healthy, they are tastier too.

The growing recipes that we have developed can be used anywhere. Green-fingered experience has been translated into digital Growing Recipes. Another important advantage: with PlantLab it is again possible to produce medicines from plants on a large scale.

Does a Plant Paradise consume a lot of energy?

Today everyone is talking about fossil energy, although there are plenty of alternatives available. The same is not true when it comes to water. Scientists expect the energy problem to be solved within one or at the most two decades, long before fossil fuels are exhausted. Within 20 to 30 years, however, water shortages will be a much greater problem. It is not possible to save more water than our system does.

The concept fits in perfectly with the trend towards Urban Farming. Will every supermarket soon have its own PlantLab?

It is conceivable that every supermarket gets its own Plant Paradise. However, things can also be done on a smaller, friendlier and more artisanal scale. A market gardener can buy a Plant Production Unit with the Growing Recipes for cucumber, tomatoes and lettuce and then set to work, either independently or with our support, to refine the recipes.

Looking at the future, what role can PlantLab play on a global scale?

We can feed the world using existing agricultural methods; we could potentially do this now and it will still be possible in 30 years time if we have 9 billion people. So the question is not whether it is possible but whether we are willing to do it using existing methods, with major global powers controlling the distribution of food. The most important factor is the availability of water. In 30 years, water supplies will be limited. At present we are very indifferent and careless in the way we manage water. Africa removes more water from the soil than its total precipitation: this is fossil water. Unless we change our agricultural methods, the struggle for water between people, nature and agriculture will become brutal during the coming decades.

How is this different from growing in a traditional greenhouse?

The key difference is that we grow without daylight, but using precisely the correct wavelengths of LED light. When it is combined with very refined climate control, this creates conditions that plants appreciate very much.

Does this meet the definition of an organic growing process?

It is much more than that. The ecological footprint of our growing method is smaller than that of existing organic methods. Just consider the amount of water consumed. Consider also the - rather short - shelf life of many regular and particularly also organic products. Our products are fresher – picked an hour ago when they were ripe for consumption – and have a longer shelf life because they have a very regular cell structure and are not damaged during transport.

What is the ultimate aim of PlantLab?

We are aiming to work with our concept in both Western countries and developing countries: Our aim is to make tasty, healthy and responsibly grown food (and decorative plants) available to local consumers and everyone else too. We would prefer to give a developing city its own nursery so that people there can grow their own food rather than offering them food aid. That is more humane and it makes more sense!

Some living creatures would prefer a world without green.

It is time to emancipate our plants.

A new building, designed like a tailor-made suit around the plant: Plant Paradise.

03 FABULOUS TO FARM

Name **Allotinabox**
URL **allotinabox.com**
Origin **United Kingdom**

grow your own vegetables in the city

An allotment is a small piece of land that is let for private gardening. You usually find them right outside the city. But land has become scarce and rent is high. So, one inspiring day in 2009, founders Gavin White and his wife Loraine, both with a strong commitment to sustainability, decided to switch careers. They moved the allotment to the city and put it in a beautifully designed, 100% recyclable and biodegradable box: Allotinabox. It is a GYO (Grow Your Own) concept to encourage the urban population to start growing fresh fruits and vegetables at home, even in the smallest spaces. Balcony, window, kitchen, rooftop, as long as you have a container, anyone from seasoned grower to first time gardener can have a go. Because there is nothing like harvesting your own food.

Allotinabox is a fairly new concept. When exactly was it founded?
The idea was conceived back in 2009. Loraine, who is my partner and co-founder ran a contemporary landscape designer agency with a specialism in small urban spaces. She noticed a shift in the way people were talking about using their spaces to grow food. After visiting a number of cities like NY, we were overwhelmed by the idea that some of the food being produced had come from local city growers and small co-operatives.

What's in a box? How does it work?
The boxes are designed to help people grow fresh produce at home. We believe that it is possible to grow food in the heart of any city. Creating a miniature edible garden is within anyone's reach and our boxes help pave the way for this. The boxes are simply purchased from our website, and then delivered to your door. They include items that help seasoned growers or complete novices to get started, such as seeds that are reflective of the season but are quite simple to start growing with. Other items include plant tags to help you or your children to identify your crops. Also, there is our famous grow wheel, which is a really handy tool that just simply enables you to identify when to sow, harvest and eat food.

What's the price of a box?
A single box is £12.99, which is great value because the yield from the seeds is quite high and it can save you money in the long run. Our boxes can also be purchased as an annual gift, 4 boxes for each season: spring, summer, autumn and winter. Each box is delivered every quarter and contains different items to help you build up your crop throughout the year. We also have specific city boxes in development, which are tailored to varieties that are easy to grow in window boxes, or on a balcony for example.

How much space do you need to get started?
A simple balcony or kitchen garden is all you need. We have customers growing in old tyres, which are fantastic for heat loving plants or herbs like Basil. The tyres heat up the soil and insulate the crop. Clever... try it and you will see!

Creating a miniature edible garden is within anyone's reach and our boxes help pave the way.

Is it an all green formula, from seed to box?

Yes, we are very conscious about the materials we use with regards to our packaging. Every item is 100% recyclable and biodegradable. Our wrapping paper can be used to make paper planting pots. The box itself can be thrown into a compost heap, although we do encourage everyone to hang onto them as they are great for storage. And everything is sourced locally from UK suppliers. Everything from our design to the sourcing of materials is within a bike ride away. So yes, Allotinabox is a product that is deeply considerate of the environment.

How would you describe the ideal Allotinabox customer? City farmer or just any one with green fingers?

Growing food should appeal to anyone. It is a great gift, not just the physical product itself, but the gift of growing food. There is deep satisfaction in knowing where your food comes from and that you have grown it from scratch and harvested the crop.

What is interesting for us is that city dwellers have really taken to the concept. It is probably because we all like to escape the buzz of the city and enjoy a bijou balcony or a little outdoor space.

Why do you want to encourage people to start growing?

We believe that it is fun, healthy and enjoyable, everyone in the family can join in. People are discovering how great it is to grow fresh fruit and vegetables. Many of our customers are young professionals with little or no experience, who are now beginning to tap into this. Most of us enjoy cooking what they have grown and we also want to get kids to understand where food comes from. Our website is helpful for anyone who wants to get started because it is not full of jargon, by just applying a few simple rules. Well, the results will be clear to see.

City farming is a hot topic. What's your opinion on the matter, trend or necessity?

Necessity... The world population is growing rapidly. More and more people are moving to cities and this will put huge pressure on food supply, the environment and transport. It is hard to believe, but over 50% of the world population now lives in cities and by 2014 it will be around 75%. That is a lot of mouths to feed. In London, there are currently around 100,000 square meters of green roofs and by the time the Olympics (2012) arrive, there will be double that amount. So, I am not surprised there is a renewed and enthusiastic interest globally.

How do you reach your customers?

We try and work with associations that are helping to change the attitude towards everything we do, from packaging and electricity consumption right through to the impact of the way we use technology. Our suppliers are also chosen because they share some of our goals, like our packaging and design which we always source locally.

We tend to get a lot of press coverage from around the world. Food bloggers like the concept and of course it is a hot topic at the moment. So, we are always connecting with journalists or businesses that are interested in working with us on projects, or that like the simplicity of the product.

In what ways can Allotinabox contribute to making our environment more sustainable? I think we already are through the eco packaging and the idea of sowing seeds which turn into food. Through our boxes anyone can grow food in cities, which in the long term helps keep them cooler. Rooftop planting helps to insulate buildings from the sun by as much as 20%. Planted areas are also better for city drainage preventing pressure on the sewers. There is a whole list of examples. We help bees pollinate. Bee keeping is thriving on London rooftops, even retailers like Harvey Nichols are getting involved! But, let us not forget that the countryside has an important role to play too, and we get some great feedback from customers who have started a kitchen garden at home and seen the benefits of growing food almost immediately.

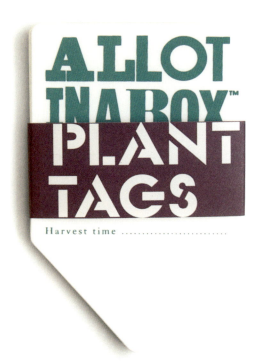
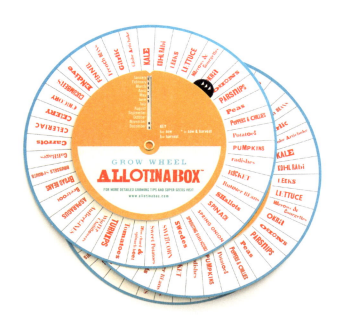

What is your goal? Where do you want to be in 5 years?

We see the brand expanding into other products, perhaps household items that are created to be highly sustainable. We are passionate about local food, so it would be fantastic to get involved in developing our own range of food. We would like to work with community partners or other organizations around the world to secure land for growing food. Actually, that is the real goal. Imagine the positive impact of using abandoned spaces and then turning them into thriving city farms. Or even just greener spaces where the community is involved and more socially aware because of it.

Creating a miniature edible garden is within anyone's reach and our boxes help pave the way.

155

04
FABULOUS TO FARM

Name **GRO Holland**
URL **gro-holland.com**
Origin **The Netherlands**

mushrooms on coffee grounds

A cradle-to-cradle concept in which organic waste is reused as the basis for a new food product is the ultimate form of sustainable, responsible enterprise. That was the aim of Dutch company GRO Mushroom, which recycles coffee grounds and transforms them into a growing medium for oyster mushrooms and other edible fungi. In July 2010 this admirable initiative resulted in a unique collaboration with restaurant chain La Place and distributor Vroegop-Windig. You can't do these things alone.

Jan Willem Bosman Jansen, the man behind GRO Mushroom:
'For me the inspiration came during a visit to Zimbabwe, where a food training programme for children and young women was being started up with assistance from the ZERI Foundation (Zero Emission Research

Initiatives). These people are learning to grow food in organic waste (which is abundantly available in their environment), immediately resulting in high-quality food. They can eat it themselves but they can also sell it, enabling them to make a living. When I got back to the Netherlands I was thinking about the opportunities that exist here. The Netherlands is another place where we have a surplus of organic waste, for example the large quantities of coffee grounds produced by espresso and other coffee machines in the hospitality sector. This enormous mountain of waste coffee can be used as the basis for a substrate suitable for growing mushrooms. Growing food in organic waste... that seems to me an ideal response to some of the problems caused by our existing economic system."

Bosman is the founder of GRO Holland, a small group of idealists who are seeking to make an active contribution towards a more sustainable economy and truly green enterprise. GRO Mushroom is part of this. At a later stage, other types of organic waste will be addressed too – there are plans to process citrus waste to make beauty products – but for now the focus is on growing mushrooms in coffee grounds. In January 2011 GRO received the first Horecava Sustainability Award.

> Why mushrooms?
> They are the most important recyclers in nature.

So why mushrooms? They are the most important recyclers in nature. They are capable of obtaining nutrition from dead or living organisms using their network of threads. In the nursery we can imitate this natural process. A substrate is made in a bag from coffee grounds and a few other organic ingredients, and mushroom spores are added to it. Within a few weeks the white threads are forming, and just 6 to 9 weeks later there are mushrooms growing outside the bags at the end of the threads. The whole process is sustainable. It begins when the coffee grounds are collected from coffee machines in restaurants. This not only means that the restaurants produce less waste, but also that the production process does not require any new raw materials. No chemical pesticides are used, either. After the harvest the substrate is passed on to tulip growers who compost it and use it to enrich the soil that they use for tulip growing. GRO could theoretically reuse the substrate itself, but that would result in smaller harvests.

You need partners to realise a concept like this. Jan Willem Bosman found them: restaurant chain La Place (www.laplace.nl) and distributor Vroegop-Windig (www.vroegop.nl). La Place is a Dutch restaurant chain with more than 120 restaurants, well known for its efforts in the area of sustainable and responsible enterprise. Vroegop-Windig is the established logistics partner of La Place. Every day this transport company delivers fresh products to all the restaurants in the Netherlands, simultaneously collects the coffee grounds and transports them directly to GRO Mushroom, where they are processed into growing substrate. The new mushroom harvest is immediately loaded up and transported back to La Place, which incorporates them in its dishes. So no unnecessary journeys are made and it all fits together perfectly. GRO Mushroom is a well thought out cradle-to-cradle concept in which the restaurant business, distributor and grower work closely together to reduce the size of their ecological footprint.

This means that the restaurants produce less waste, but also that the production process does not require any new raw materials.

05 FABULOUS TO FARM

Name Willem & Drees
URL willemendrees.nl
Origin The Netherlands

fresh potatoes, vegetables and fruit from local farmer to supermarket

Supermarkets transport vegetables and fruit from the other side of the world, while local farmers cannot find a market for their products. The world seems upside down, but that is how it usually works. The Netherlands was no exception in that respect. Until in 2009 Willem Treep and Drees Peter van den Bosch decided that something had to change and found the missing link that could bring the two closer together. At Willem&Drees they make sure that farm fresh seasonal products do find their way to local supermarkets or greengrocers. It was a leap in the dark. They were sure of their concept, but how do you persuade a supermarket to throw over a system that is 'working perfectly well'? Two years later they are growing so fast it is hard to keep up.

In 2011 they are working with 70 growers and over 200 stores in the Netherlands have a Willem&Drees counter. Eventually they want to have eight hundred. You can recognise the concept from the bare wooden boxes in which the fresh products are presented, with the Willem&Drees logo and the words 'direct from the farmer' ('rechtstreeks van de boer'). The name of the grower and the place of origin are displayed on each product. That gives consumers a sense of confidence, as if they could just pop in and see the farmer. In fact they can do so, because the farmer always lives within a 40 km (25 miles) radius of the store.

How exactly did the concept come into being?

Willem&Drees was born out of a sense of amazement that the apples from the farmer around the corner were not for sale in our neighbourhood. One day Drees spoke to a farmer who was complaining because he was unable to sell his apples. At the same time there was a special offer at Albert Heijn supermarket for the new harvest of Elstar apples. "Nice", thought Drees. Until he discovered that the Elstar apples were from France, not the Netherlands. Supermarkets prefer products that can be delivered all the year round in large volumes. That automatically excludes local growers who follow the seasons and produce limited volumes. We wanted to change that. Although it may seem attractive to be able to buy the same fresh products all the year round, it is definitely not sustainable and it also alienates us from the food on our plates.

What approach did you use to get the supermarkets on board?

It was quite a tense time, because we had no idea whether the supermarkets would be open to our idea. We went to the supermarkets, explained our idea, told them that we were starting on 1 June (2009) and asked them if they wanted to join in. After one or two had taken the plunge, the rest followed. In one year we have gone from 10 to more than 100 stores.

Gert and Annette Verweij's potatoes from Leusden

Else Schimmel's lettuce from Voorthuizen

Arie Verheij's strawberries from Lopikerkapel

Toon Vernooij's pears from Cothen

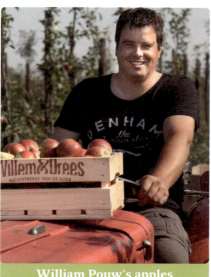
William Pouw's apples from Schalkwijk

Gerjan Snippe's cauliflower from Zeewolde

Thijmen Van Voorthuizen's cherries from Terschuur

Jan van Geffen's forgotten vegetables from Lelystad

What we like best is the pride that you see in those farmers. They are proud of their farm, proud of their products and proud of their family and workers.

Sustainability was the starting-point. We wanted to create something that would help to build a better world.

Andre Jurrius' onions from Randwijk

Frederik and Marian Bunt's plums from Slijk-Ewijk

Chris Kempenaar's coloured carrots from Leimuiden

Dennis van de Weerd's black salsify roots from Lelystad

Hessel Bierma's French beans from Biddinghuizen

Wim Schoemaker's carrots from Warmsveld

Rob van Paassen's vegetables from Oude Leede

Gaveshi Reus' asparagus from Groeningen

We stick to the lesson that Michael Pollan taught us: "Shake the hand that feeds you."

How do you divide up the work?

I contact the stores and do the marketing. Drees is responsible for the growers and logistics. Initially the whole logistics process was managed by an outside company, but we moved away from that quite quickly. Now we do everything ourselves. The products are collected from the growers by our drivers each morning and brought to the stores via a regional distribution centre. The driver also makes sure everything is placed neatly on the shelves.

What added value do you get from locally grown products?

Of course the added value has to be in the form of tasty, high-quality products. Nevertheless, it does go beyond that. We want to show people what the seasons are, the specific products that come from each individual region and, most importantly of all, we want to restore the link between the people who produce the food and the people who eat it. If a grower knows that his consumers live just round the corner from him and the consumer knows that he can get in touch with a grower in his own locality, that creates a natural balance so that the consumer is willing to pay an honest price and the grower wants to grow a high-quality, sustainable product. One result is that growers will try to stand out by offering specific products and different varieties. For example, we have brought organic sprouts on the stalk back into the shops. A whole stalk like that creates a closer link to the product than a plastic bag containing 500 grammes of cleaned sprouts.

Aren't your products more expensive?

We are not more expensive for consumers, but we do have some special products that command higher prices. The store makes do with smaller margins and because there are no other parties in between, there are less margins stacking up along the chain. The margin is distributed along the chain like this: the consumer price is 106, so that is 100 excluding VAT. The retailer's margin is 30. So Willem&Drees sells for 70. Our margin is 25. The ultimate price for the grower is 45. So the grower receives much more from Willem&Drees; in a conventional chain they get about 23%.

To what extent has sustainability played a part from the beginning?

Sustainability was the starting-point. We wanted to create something that would help to build a better world. Fresh seasonal potatoes, vegetables and fruit, from the farmer to the plate without travelling unnecessary miles - that is a sustainable way to live.

What I find intriguing in the debate about sustainability is that we often focus on details that do not really make a difference. We could make a much greater impact if a large part of the population could keep in mind a few simple rules and simply adjust their everyday behaviour accordingly.

How do you select your growers? Are they always organic farmers?

We select growers by going to see them and getting a feel for the way they approach their life and work. We stick to the lesson that Michael Pollan taught us: "Shake the hand that feeds you." By meeting and getting to know the people who produce your food, you can gain real insights into the choices that they have made. That leads to understanding and confidence. You can use this to build up a lasting relationship that is based on working together. I do often notice that individual growers have their own preferences, and that is what is so important. If they are really putting their heart into growing a product, that will result in higher quality and it will give us a better story to tell too. They are often organic farmers, but it is not a requirement. The way organic farmers operate usually matches our own way of working, but we also believe in good growers who try to find a better balance between quality, production and the environment every day. What we like best is the pride that you see in those farmers. They are proud of their farm, proud of their products and proud of their family and workers.

How do you see Willem&Drees evolving in the future?

Willem&Drees wants to allow people to discover extraordinary products from their own locality. We would like to carry on doing that forever, because discovering things is wonderful. Every day we are finding that more and more people want to know more about their food - and the trend is accelerating. People no longer simply believe in the ideas that the big players are trying to sell us. They are looking for smaller-scale initiatives run by people who are honestly trying their hardest to come up with a great product. In the end their genuine passion does come through, and people are willing to pay for that.

> We could make a much greater impact if a large part of the population could keep in mind a few simple rules and simply adjust their everyday behaviour accordingly.

Credits

FABULOUS FOOD CONCEPTS

respecting the planet

Production
Sigrid Vandensavel

Interviews
Sigrid Vandensavel
Karoline Neujens
Marc Verhagen

Translation Miles Translations

Graphic Design Touch De Clercq

Special thanks to Jan Vannoppen (Velt) for contributing to the introduction.

D/2011/12.005/24
ISBN 9789460580789
NUR 802
© 2011 Luster, Antwerp
www.lusterweb.com

All rights reserved.

No part of this publication may be reproduced, stored in a retrieval system, or transmitted, in any form or by any

means, without the prior written consent of the publisher. An exception is made for short excerpts which may be cited

for the sole purpose of reviews.

Photo credits

COVER

Outstanding in the Field © Jeremy Fenske

FABULOUS TO GO

Leon © Georgia Glynn Smith
(glynnsmith.co.uk)

Burgermeester
portrait © Annemiek van den Broek
photos restaurant © Burgermeester
art work © Menno Endt (crookedline.nl)

Soepmie
portrait © Debby Huysmans
(debbyhuysmans.be)
other photos & art work © Soepmie

Kickstand
photos left © Jack Shanahan
(jackshanahan.com)
photos right © Kickstand

Outstanding in the Field
portrait © Jamin Townsley
other photos © Jeremy Fenske

Marije Vogelzang © marije vogelzang

De Kas
P 42 © De Kas
other photos © Ronald Hoeben
(ronaldhoeben.com)

Dogmatic
photos and art work © Mother New York
(mothernewyork.com)

Le Pain Quotidien © Le Pain Quotidien
– PQ Licensing, SA

FABULOUS TO BUY

Y water © Y water

Bee Raw Honey © Sam Yocum

Original Beans © Original Beans

Dry Soda © Dry Soda

BOS Ice tea
portrait & packshots © Pete Maltbie
photos klipopmekaar © Daniel Naudé
(danielnaude.com)

Frozen Dutch
Portrait © Eric van Lokven
(ericvanlokven.com)
other photos © Simon Wald Lasowski
(simonwaldlasowski.com)

Tap water™ © tap water™

LunchSkins © LunchSkins

WB&CO © Olivier Henry
(milkphotograpie.com)

FABULOUS TO SHOP

Marqt
p 107 © Kees Hummel (keeshummel.com)
other photos © Labl.Photography (labl.nl)

The People's Supermarket © Haarala
Hamilton Photography
(haaralahamilton.com)

Unpackaged
portrait © the-hub.net

p117 and p 119 below © Suzy Tuxen
(multistorey.net)
other photos © John Carey (john-carey.com)

Fishes
p 123 © Fred Greaves (fredgreaves.com)
packshots © Daniel Patriasz
(danielpatriasz.nl)
interior photos of the shop © teo krijgsman
(teokrijgsman.nl)
other photos © Chris Arend
(chrisarendphoto.com)

De Vegetarische Slager © De
Vegetarische Slager

Mutterland
portrait, p 132 below and p 135 above ©
Thilo Schoch (thiloschoch.de)
other photos © Mutterland

Lindy & Grundy
photos © Jennifer May (jennifermay.com)

photo **Brooklyn Grange Farm**
p 140-141 © Cyrus Dowlatshahi
(cyrusdowlatshahi.com)

FABULOUS TO FARM

Dakboerin
portrait © David Galjaard (davidgaljaard.nl)
other photos © annelies kuyper

PlantLab © Lex van Lieshout

Allotinabox © Allotinabox™

GRO Holland © GRO Holland

Willem&Drees © Willem&drees